the STORY of the WORLD

Volume 1: Ancient Times

STUDENT WORKBOOK

25th Anniversary Expanded Edition

the STORY of the WORLD

Volume 1: Ancient Times

From the Earliest Nomads to the Last Roman Emperor

STUDENT WORKBOOK

25th Anniversary Expanded Edition

Edited by Susan Wise Bauer, Susanna Jarrett, and Kat Stelly

WELL-TRAINED MIND PRESS

www.welltrainedmind.com

A Note to Parents (Preview Notice)

Please preview the coloring pages for chapters 19, 23, and 31 (Student Pages 59, 76, and 99), to make sure that they are appropriate for your family.

Publisher's Cataloging-in-Publication
(Provided by Cassidy Cataloguing Services, Inc.)

Title: Student workbook : Story of the world. Vol. 1, Ancient times.
Other titles: Story of the world. Vol. 1, Ancient times : student workbook
Description: 25th anniversary expanded edition. | Charles City, Virginia : Well-Trained Mind Press, [2026] | Series: Bauer, Susan Wise. Story of the world. | Interest grade level: 1-4.
Identifiers: ISBN: 9781944481872 (paperback)
Subjects: LCSH: World history--Problems, exercises, etc. | Civilization--Problems, exercises, etc. | History, Ancient--Problems, exercises, etc. | Nomads--History--Problems, exercises, etc. | LCGFT: Problems and exercises. | BISAC: EDUCATION / Home Schooling. | EDUCATION / Schools / Levels / Elementary. | EDUCATION / Teaching / Subjects / Arts & Humanities.
Classification: LCC: D20 .B35 2026 | DDC: 909--dc23

Table of Contents

Narration Page

Name: ______________________________ Chapter: __________

A HISTORY OF ______________________________

____
Birth Date

____
City, State, and Country of Birth

____
Father's Name (if known)

____
Mother's Name (if known)

Tape picture
or drawing
here

INTERVIEW QUESIONS

1. Tell me about where you lived growing up. ______________________________

____

2. What is your favorite memory? ______________________________

____

3. ______________________________

____

4. ______________________________

____

5. ______________________________

____

Name ______________________

Date ______________________

The First Nomads

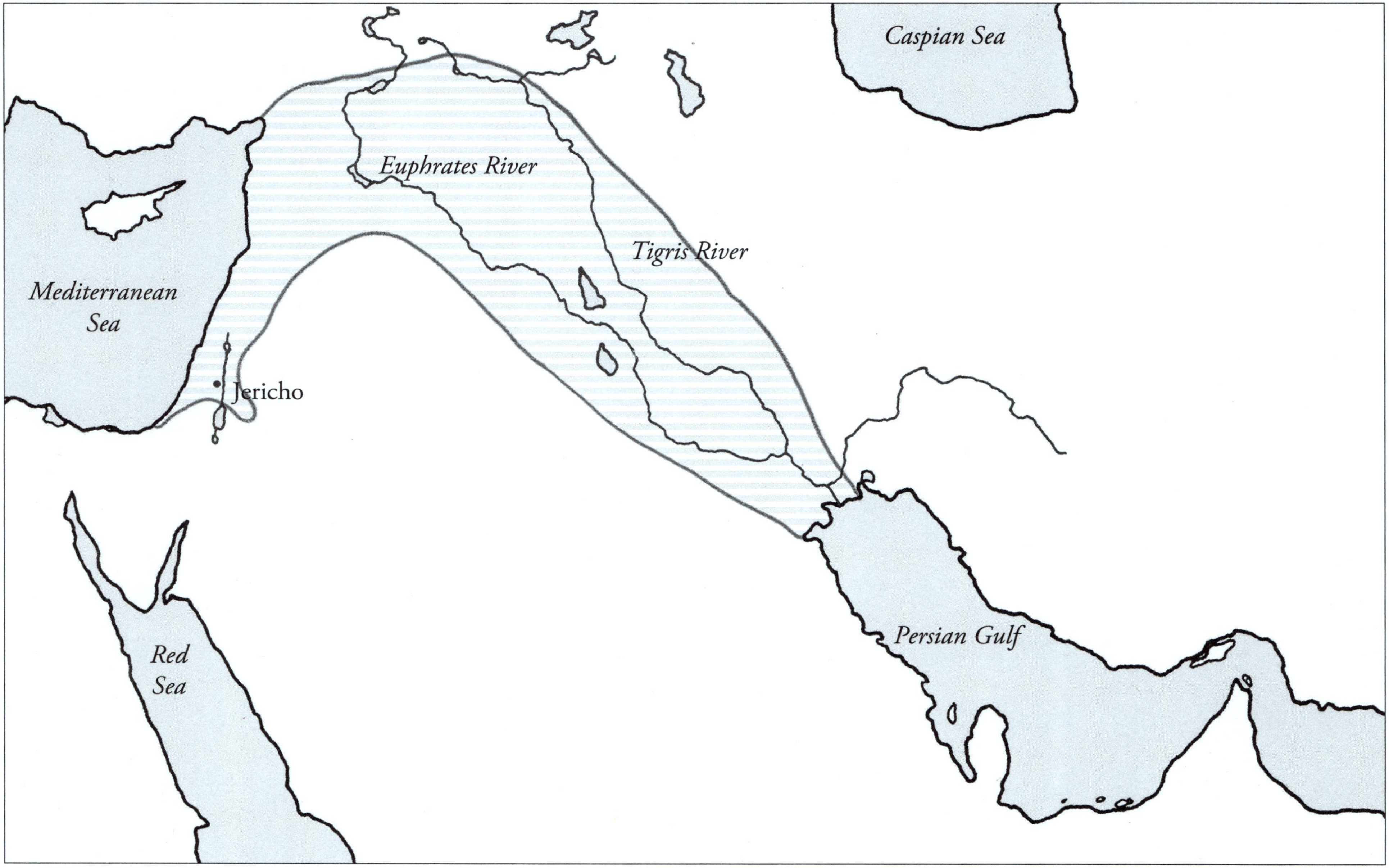

A Farmer Using a Shaduf

Name ______________________________ Date ______________

Two Kingdoms Become One

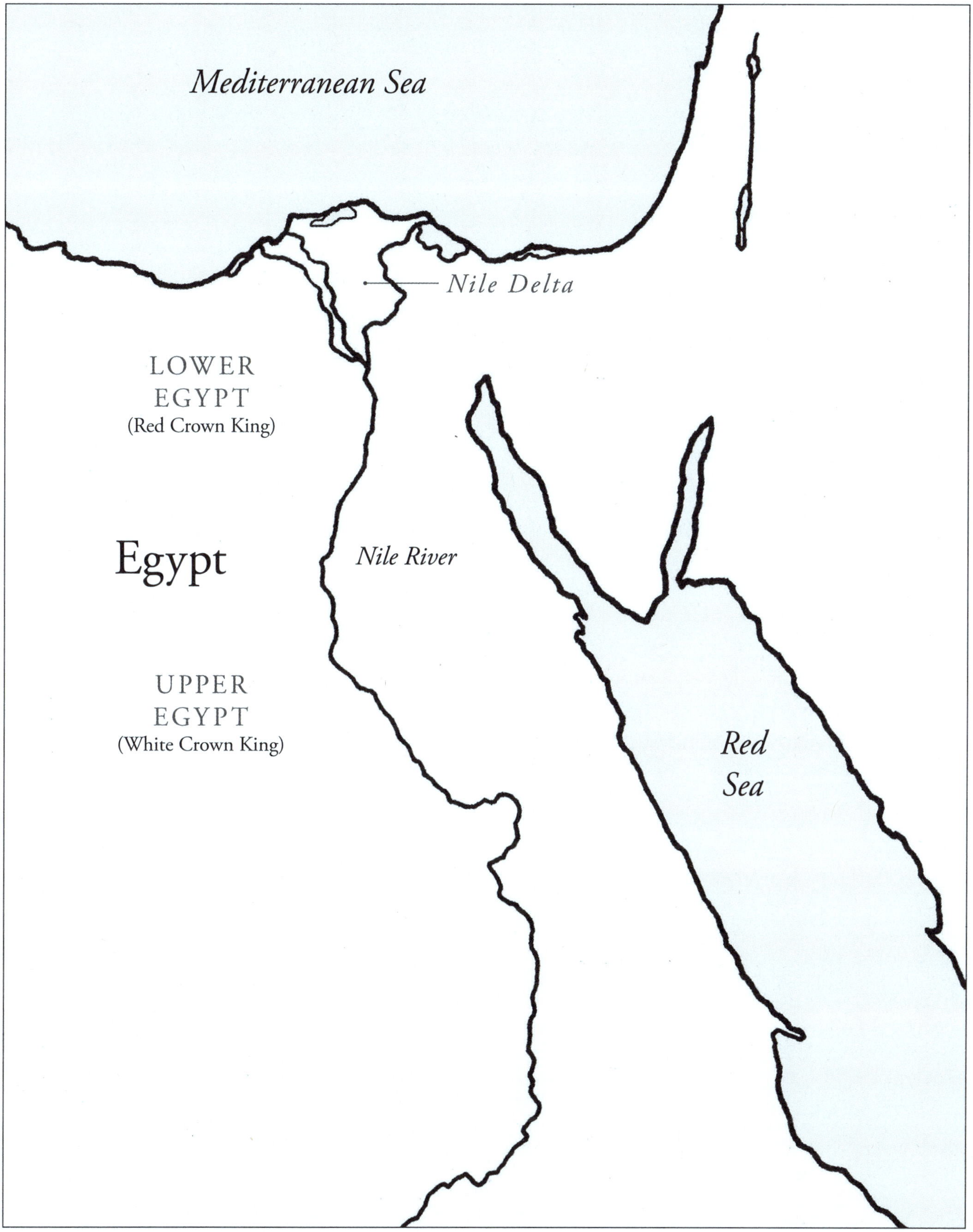

Osiris and Set

RA

Sun God

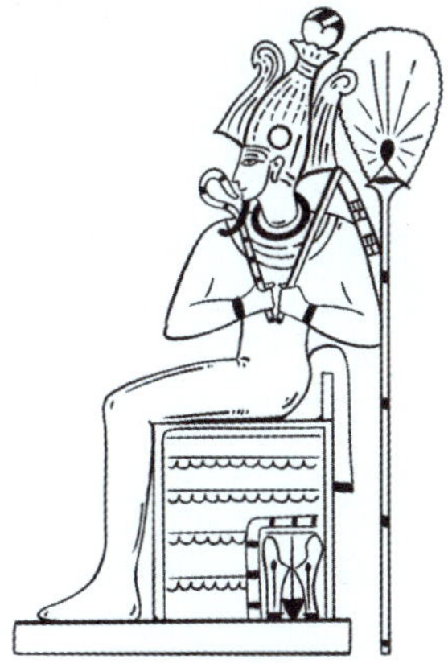

OSIRIS

God of the Underworld

ISIS

Mother Goddess

SET

God of Chaos

HATHOR

Goddess of Love, Beauty, and Music

ANUBIS

God of Mummification and the Afterlife

THOTH

God of Writing and Wisdom

HORUS

God of the Sky

BASTET

Goddess of Cats and Motherhood

Name ______________________________ Date ____________

The First Writing

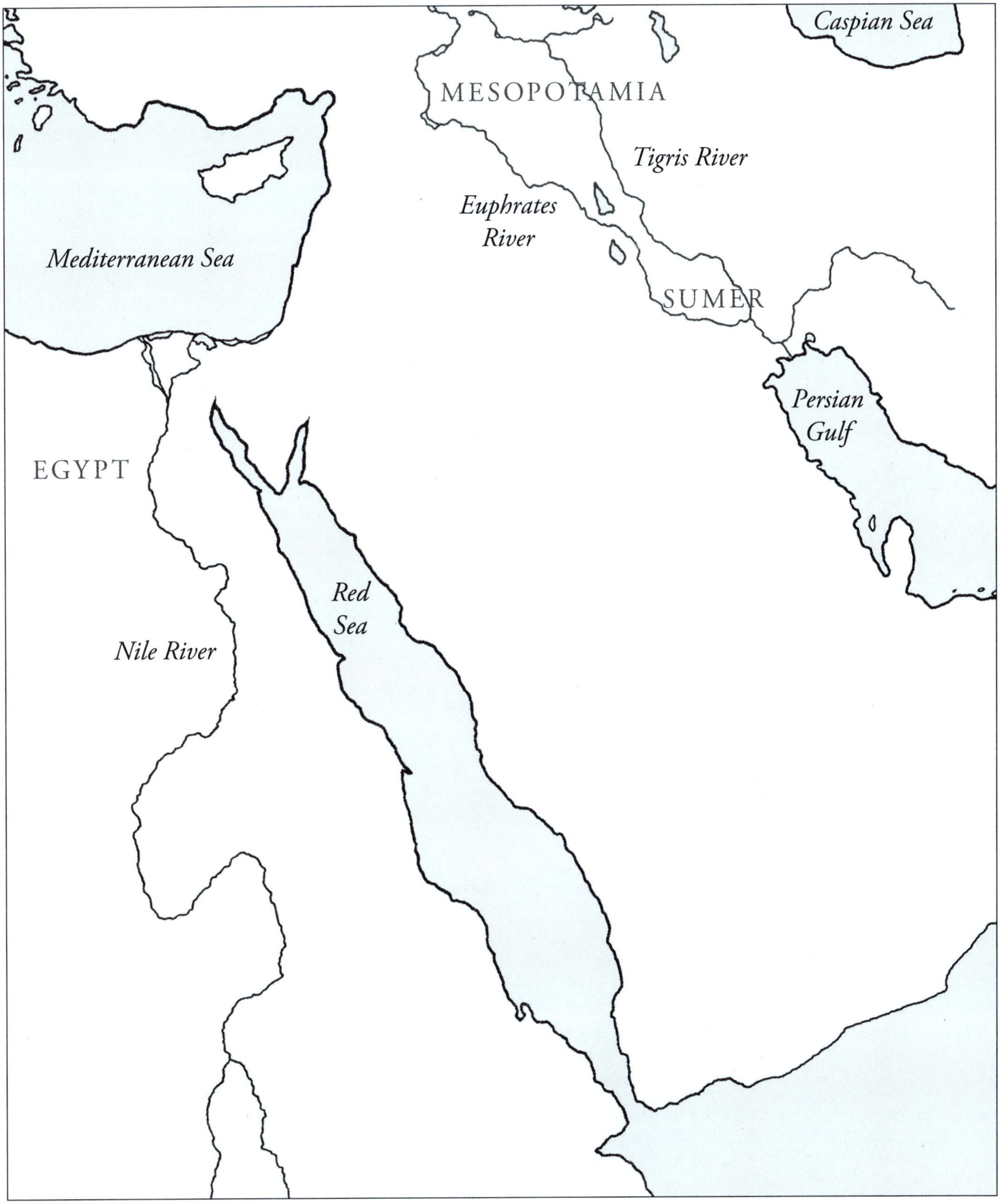

Carving Hieroglyphs

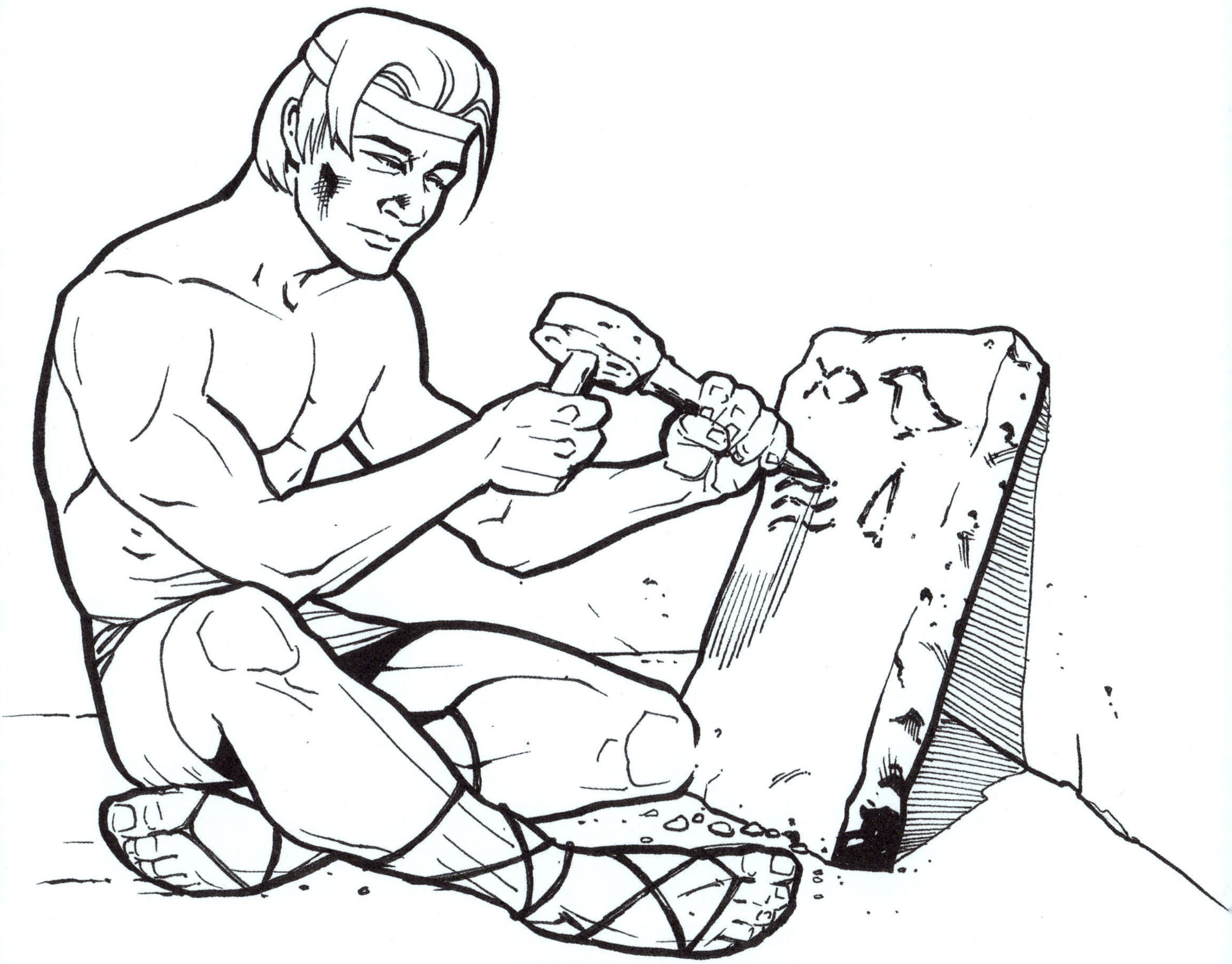

Cuneiform Chart

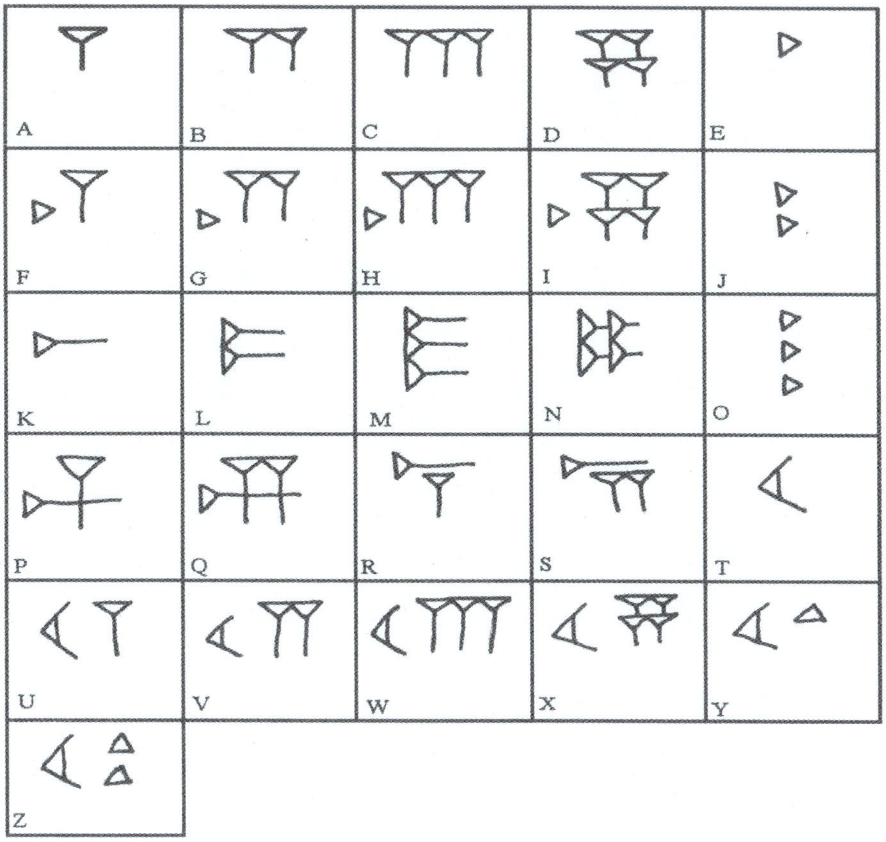

Hieroglyph Chart

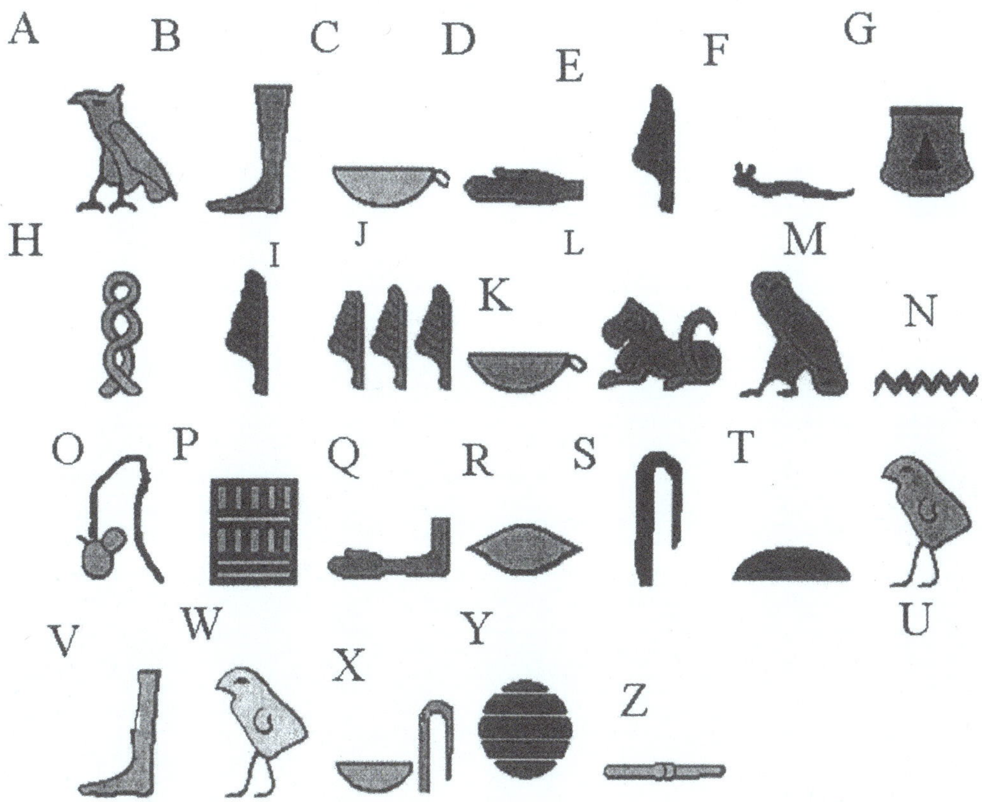

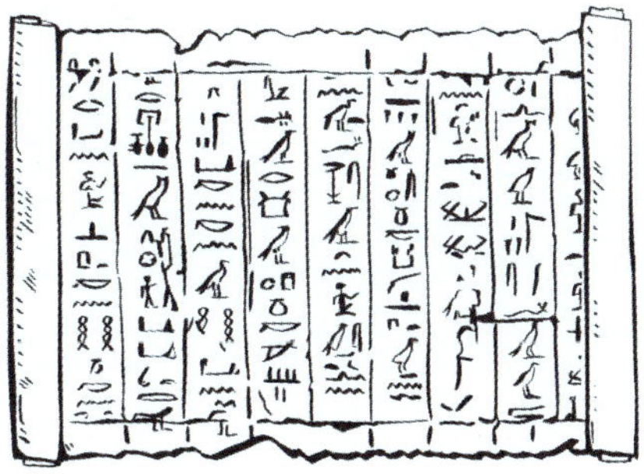 

Flood		
Desert		
Extended Use How many times did you unroll your scroll? ____________________		
Fire (optional)		

Key: ✓ = not damaged, ☹ = damaged, ✗ = destroyed.

Name ______________________________ Date ____________

Egyptian Pyramids

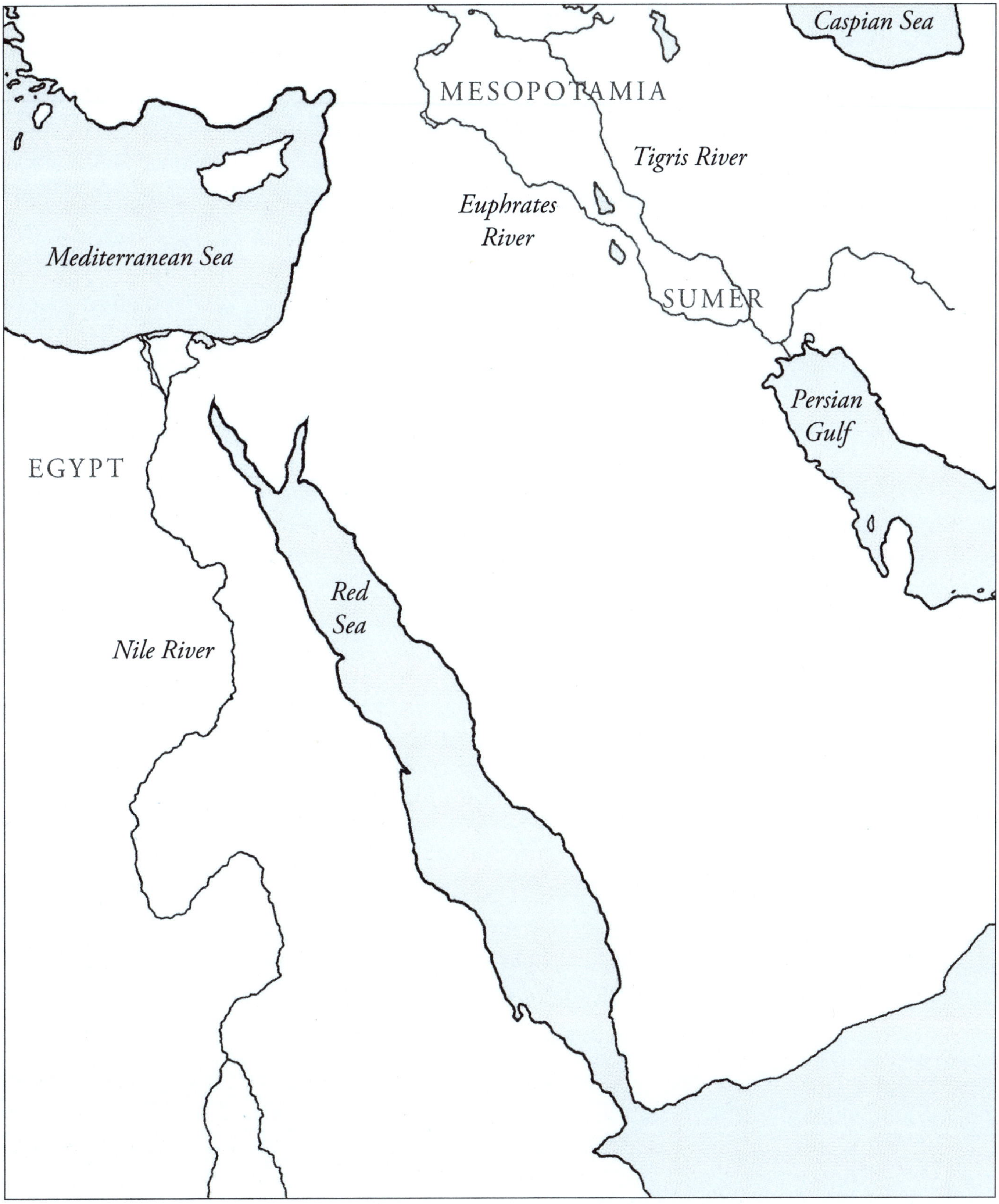

The Pyramids of Egypt

Sargon and the Akkadians

Name ______________________

Date ______________________

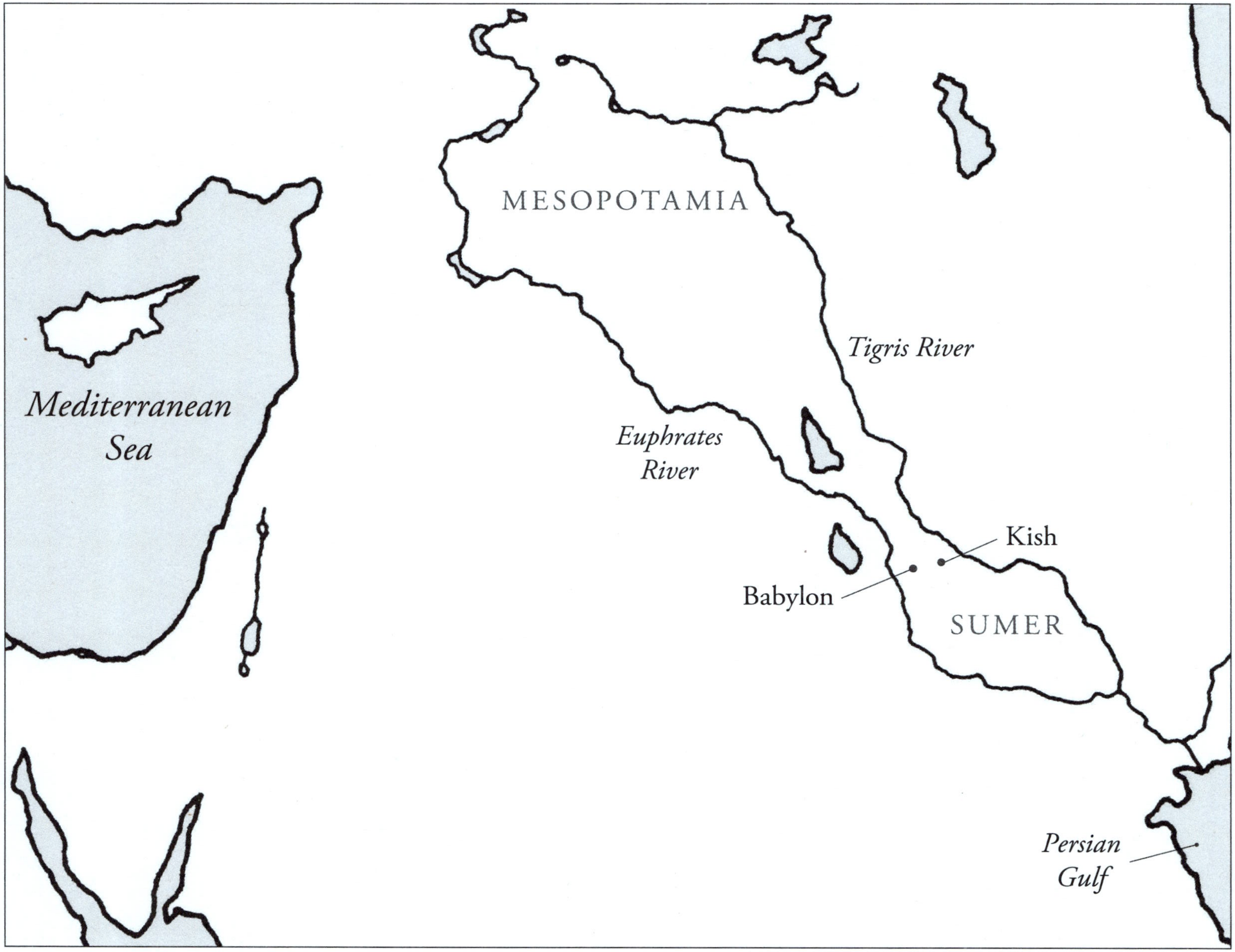

Sargon

King of Mesopotamia

Sumerian Inventions Word Search

Find the following hidden words. The words may be written from left to right, from top to bottom, or diagonally.

wheel, shaduf, clock, pottery, hour, numbers,
minute, calendar, cuneiforms, sumer

N	E	M	R	V	S	U	M	E	R	J	P
G	R	A	N	H	H	A	R	F	N	B	R
A	W	E	U	Y	A	A	L	N	K	T	I
E	H	I	M	I	D	R	P	C	S	T	A
K	E	N	B	N	U	E	O	E	S	C	E
Z	E	G	E	F	F	L	T	S	O	I	M
O	L	L	R	R	C	U	T	H	S	P	L
E	A	L	S	T	N	N	E	G	N	H	T
C	U	N	E	I	F	O	R	M	S	V	R
Z	T	T	M	T	C	U	Y	E	C	O	H
N	H	M	P	G	O	R	E	U	D	S	E
F	D	E	E	H	O	S	U	E	K	G	S

The Ziggurat of Ur

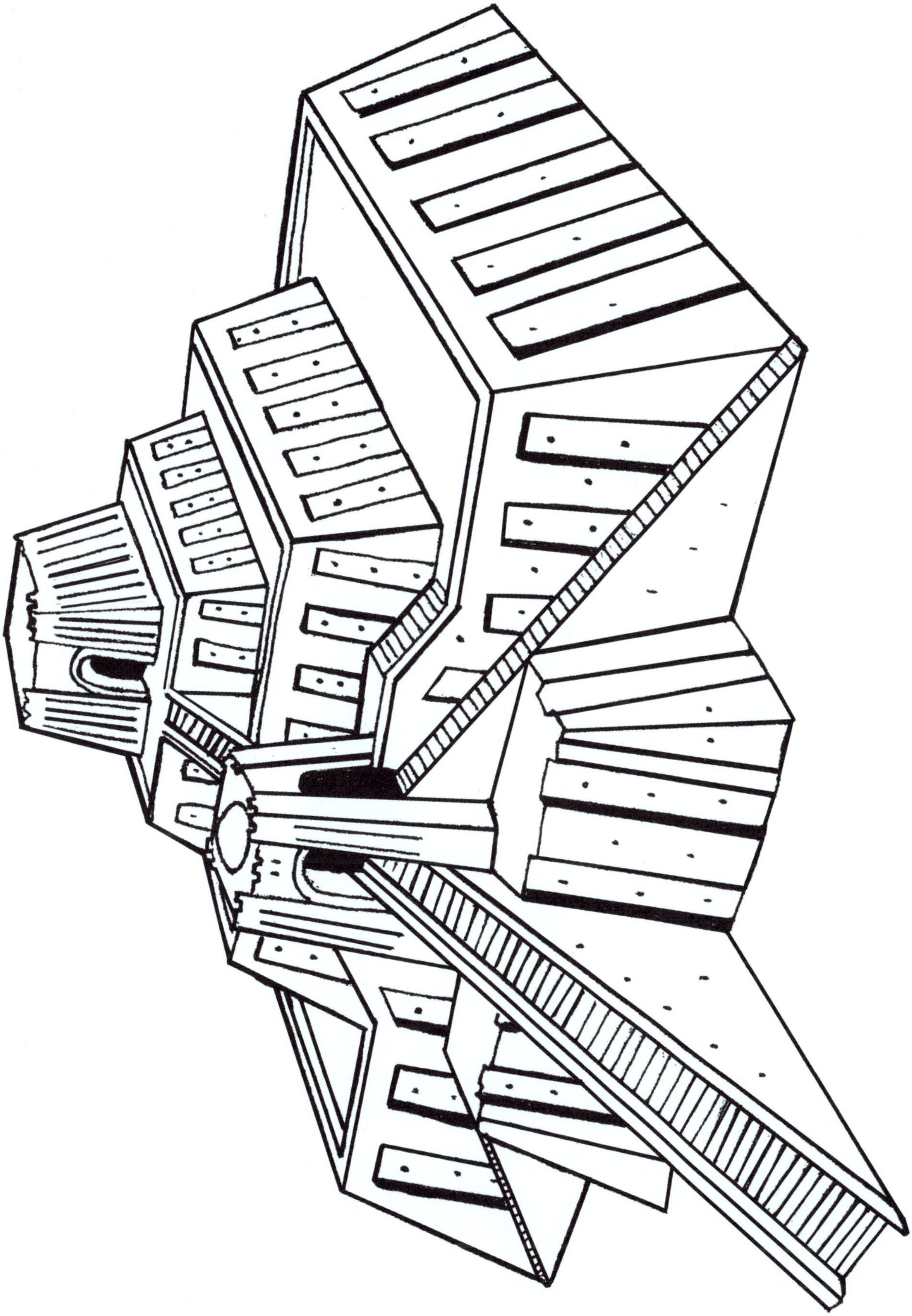

Joseph Goes to Egypt

Name ______________________

Date ______________________

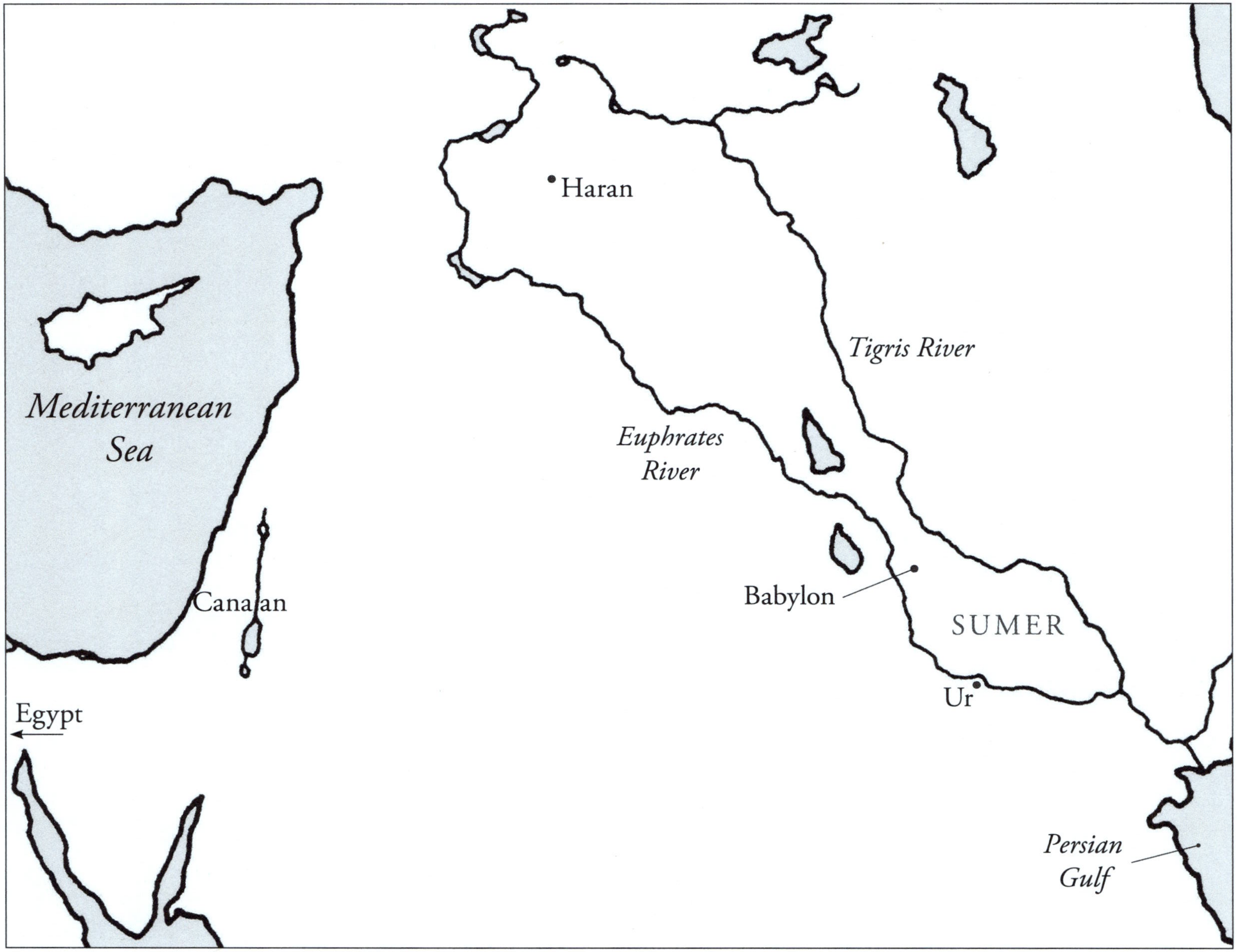

The Jewish People Word Search

Directions:

1. Solve the following clues, and write the answers in the spaces provided.
2. All the answer words from the clues are in the word search and run from left to right, top to bottom, or diagonally. Find them now.

Clues:

1. Sargon the Great was a ruler of this river-side city-state where Terah and his family first lived. _ _
2. The name of Abram's father. _ _ _ _ _
3. The threat of war with Babylon caused Terah to decide to move from his hometown. He and his family moved to what merchant town? _ _ _ _ _
4. Once they moved, Abram looked after the sheep, goats and cattle. What is another name for cattle? _ _ _ _
5. When Terah died, Abram was advised by his one god to move to this new location. _ _ _ _ _ _
6. Abram's new-found god renamed both Abram and his wife. Abram's wife was renamed this. _ _ _ _ _
7. Abram's new name was this. _ _ _ _ _ _ _
8. Abram laughed at his god when he was told he would have a baby with his wife. When she did have that baby, they named him this, because it means "laughter." _ _ _ _ _
9. Their son, had a son named this. _ _ _ _ _
10. Jacob had twelve sons. Which was his favorite? _ _ _ _ _ _
11. Jacob made this special, colorful piece of clothing for his favorite son. _ _ _ _
12. Because of the envy his brothers felt, they sold Joseph to be this. _ _ _ _ _
13. Joseph was taken to this country. _ _ _ _ _
14. While in prison, Joseph demonstrated his ability to tell the meaning of something we think about while we're sleeping. He knew what a _ _ _ _ _ meant.
15. Later, someone had a dream about seven fat cows that were eaten by seven thin cows. Who had this dream? _ _ _ _ _ _ _
16. Joseph knew the Pharaoh's dream meant that seven good years would be followed by seven years of famine. To help the people, he suggested they collect this in each of the seven good years, so there would be enough during the dry years. _ _ _ _ _

The Jewish People Word Search

J	A	C	O	B	E	T	S	M	D	R	E	A	M	F
C	B	A	O	L	R	R	I	N	R	U	T	X	C	G
R	R	N	X	A	B	E	F	E	E	L	Y	B	O	A
E	A	A	K	R	T	Z	U	D	P	E	G	Y	P	T
T	H	A	R	A	N	C	H	G	H	R	N	C	E	E
T	A	N	R	S	F	D	J	P	A	T	I	V	B	R
H	M	S	L	A	V	E	O	S	R	I	H	S	Y	A
I	S	A	A	C	O	W	S	A	A	U	W	R	O	H
N	S	A	R	A	H	P	E	R	O	G	R	A	I	N
D	Y	V	G	X	W	R	P	H	H	D	I	K	F	P
R	O	Y	E	Q	I	O	H	L	F	P	A	G	E	Y

If you have difficulty answering the clues on the previous page, see if you can find the right word from this list: ABRAHAM, CANAAN, COAT, COWS, DREAM, EGYPT, GRAIN, HARAN, ISAAC, JACOB, JOSEPH, PHARAOH, SARAH, SLAVE, TERAH, UR

REUBEN	DAN	ISSACHAR
SIMEON	NAPHTALI	ZEBULUN
LEVI (THE PRIESTS)	GAD	JOSEPH — OR — EPHRAIM AND MANASSEH
JUDAH	ASHER	BENJAMIN

Hammurabi's Code

Name ____________________

Date ____________________

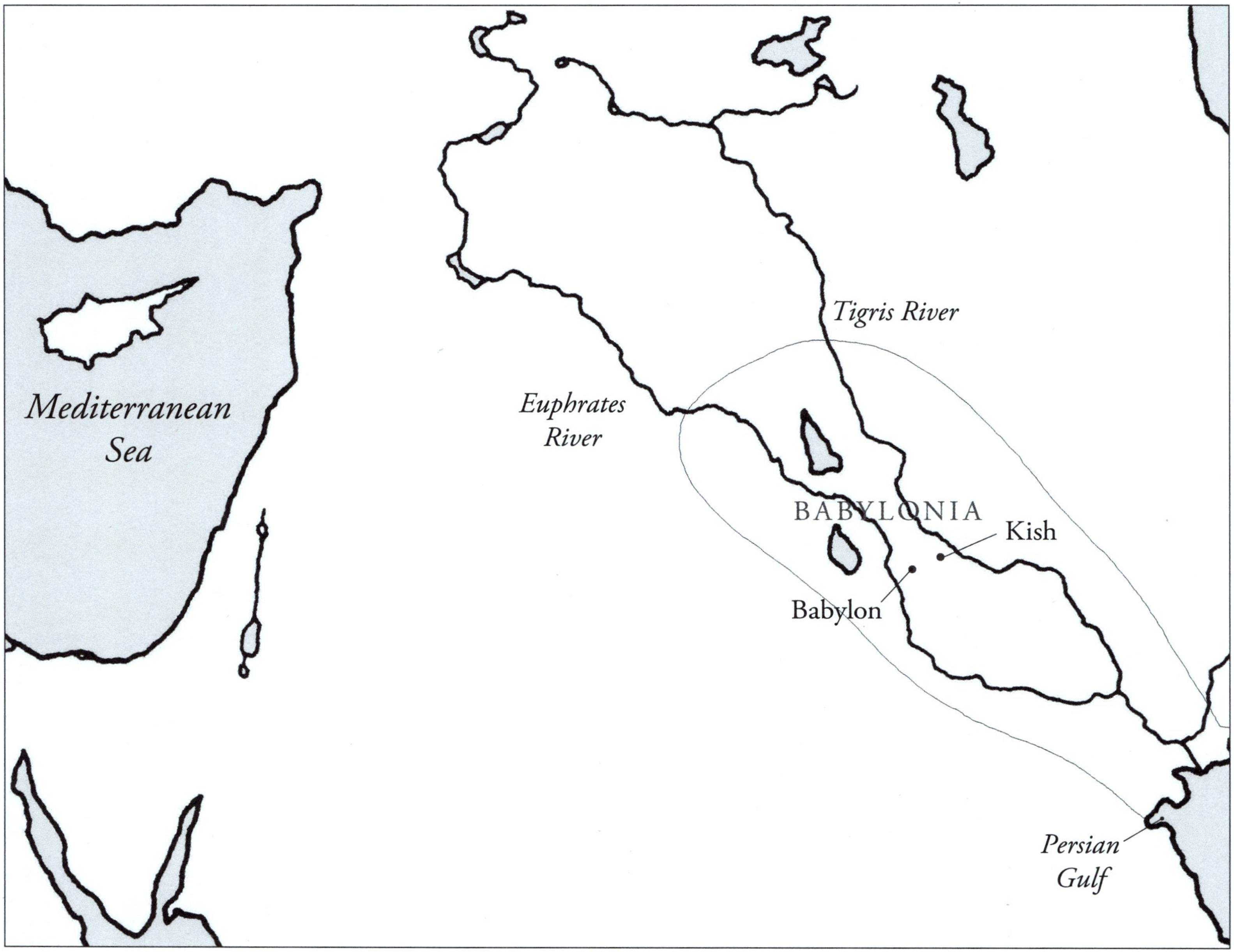

Crossword Puzzle: Name That Place

Across

3. The name Sargon called his new kingdom
4. The town Abraham was from
6. The name of one of the first cities in the world

Down

1. The name of Hammurabi's city
2. Not the Euphrates River; the other one
5. The name of the city where Sargon first lived

SCENARIO 1:

Ki hired someone to help build him a house. The builder finished the project, but didn't do a good job. The walls are crooked and have begun to crack. What should happen?

PUNISHMENT 1:

If a builder builds a house and the walls are not straight, he must rebuild it with his own money.

SCENARIO 2:

Enki took his father to a doctor for a major surgery. During the surgery, Enki's father died from an incision that the doctor made. What should happen?

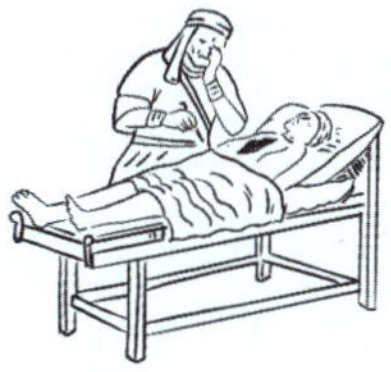

PUNISHMENT 2:

If a doctor makes an incision for surgery and the patient dies, the doctor's hand will be cut off.

SCENARIO 3:

Arlu owes his relative Ereshkigal a sum of money. Ereshkigal asked for the money, but Arlu does not have the funds to pay him back. What should happen?

PUNISHMENT 3:

If a man cannot pay his debts he must sell his wife, son, or daughter into service. After four years, they shall be given their freedom.

SCENARIO 4:

Utu and Ishtar are friends, but they got into a fight and Utu broke Ishtar's arm. What should happen?

PUNISHMENT 4:

If a man breaks the bone of his equal, he shall have his bone broken.

SCENARIO 5:

Hazi did not want to work on his cuneiform. His father forced him to complete his work. Hazi became angry and slapped his father on the face. What should happen?

PUNISHMENT 5:

If a boy hits his father, his hand should be cut off.

SCENARIO 6:

Zua claims that Tilar stole his cow. Tilar claims that the cow belonged to him all along. He says that Zua's cow died and that is why Zua wants his cow. Nobody knows the truth. What should happen?

PUNISHMENT 6:

If an accused man jumps into the river and dies, the accuser may take possession of his house. If he survives, the accuser shall be executed and the accused shall take possession of his house.

Scenario:	My fair punishment:	Hammurabi's Code:
Scenario 1 		
Scenario 2 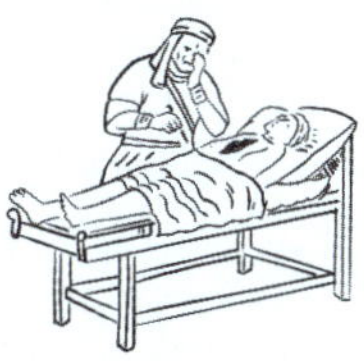		
Scenario 3 		
Scenario 4 		
Scenario 5 		
Scenario 6 		

Shamshi-Adad, King of the Whole World

Name ______________________

Date ______________________

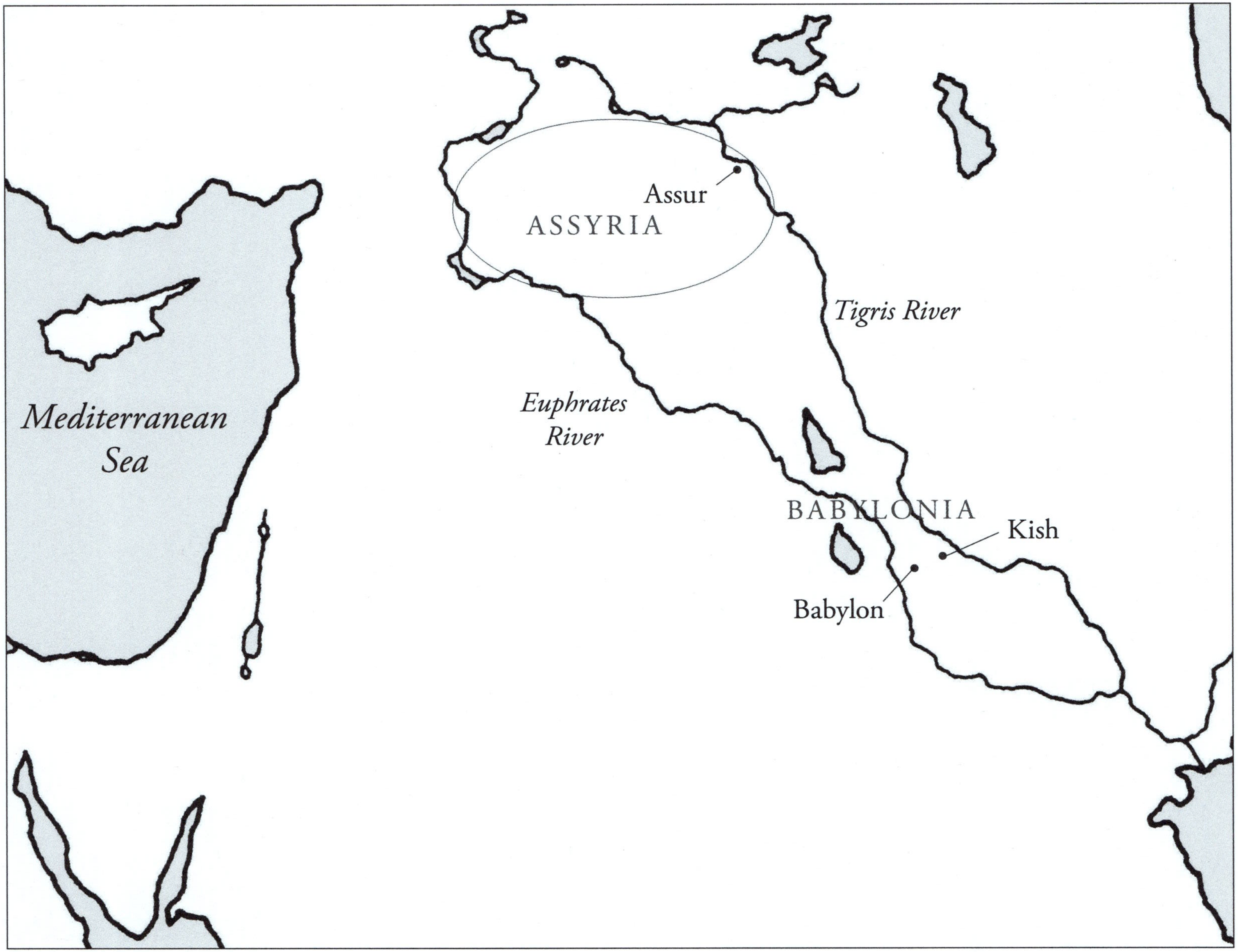

Gilgamesh and the Lion

1. Tigris and Euphrates - Mesopotamia
2. Nile - Egypt
3. Indus River - Indus Valley Civilization or Harappan Civilization
4. Yellow River - (Ancient China)
5. Ganges River - Mauryan Empire

The Mystery of Mohenjo-Daro

Name ____________________

Date ____________________

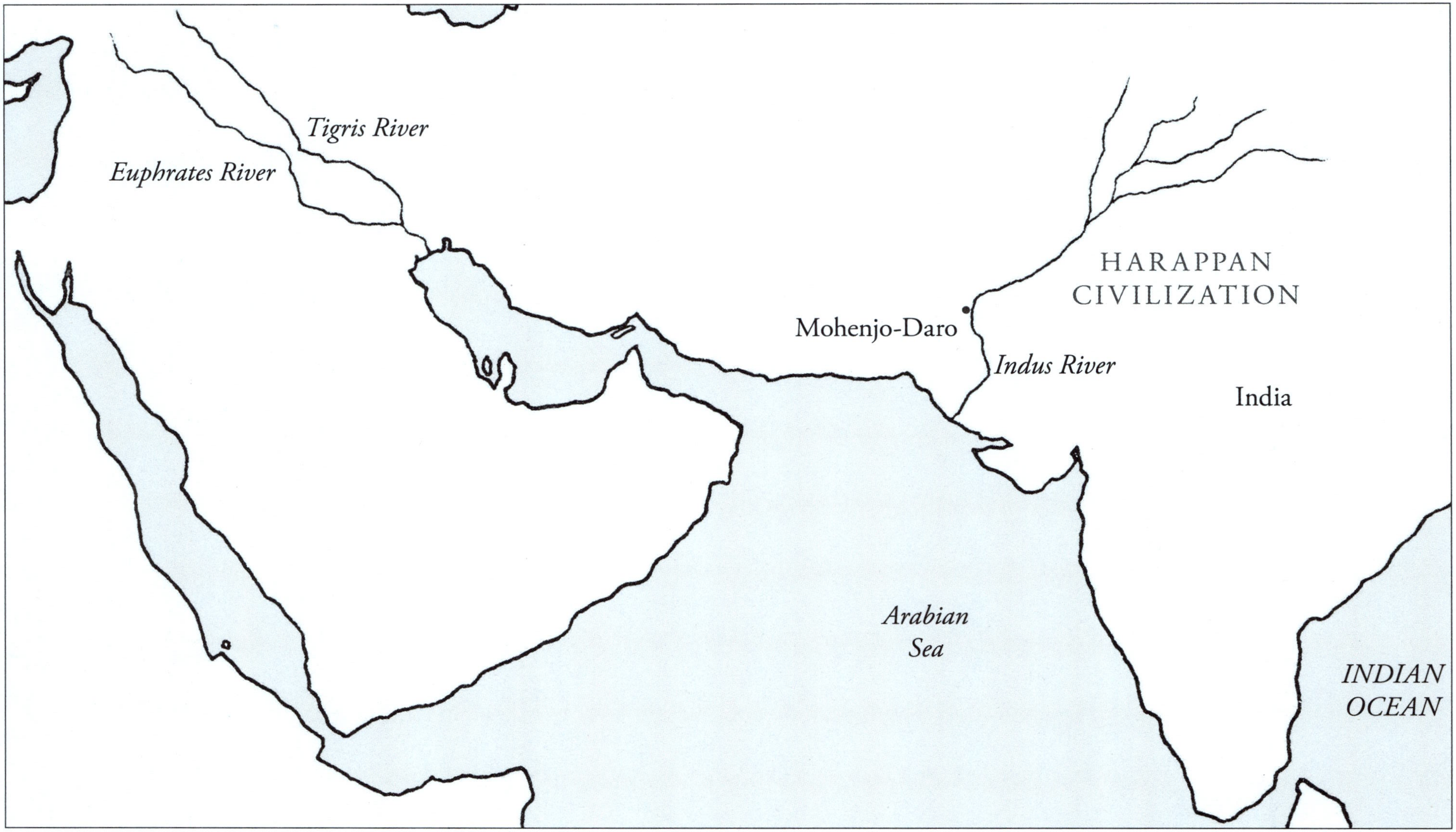

A Statue From Mohenjo-Daro

Lei Zu and the Silkworm

Name ______________________

Date ______________________

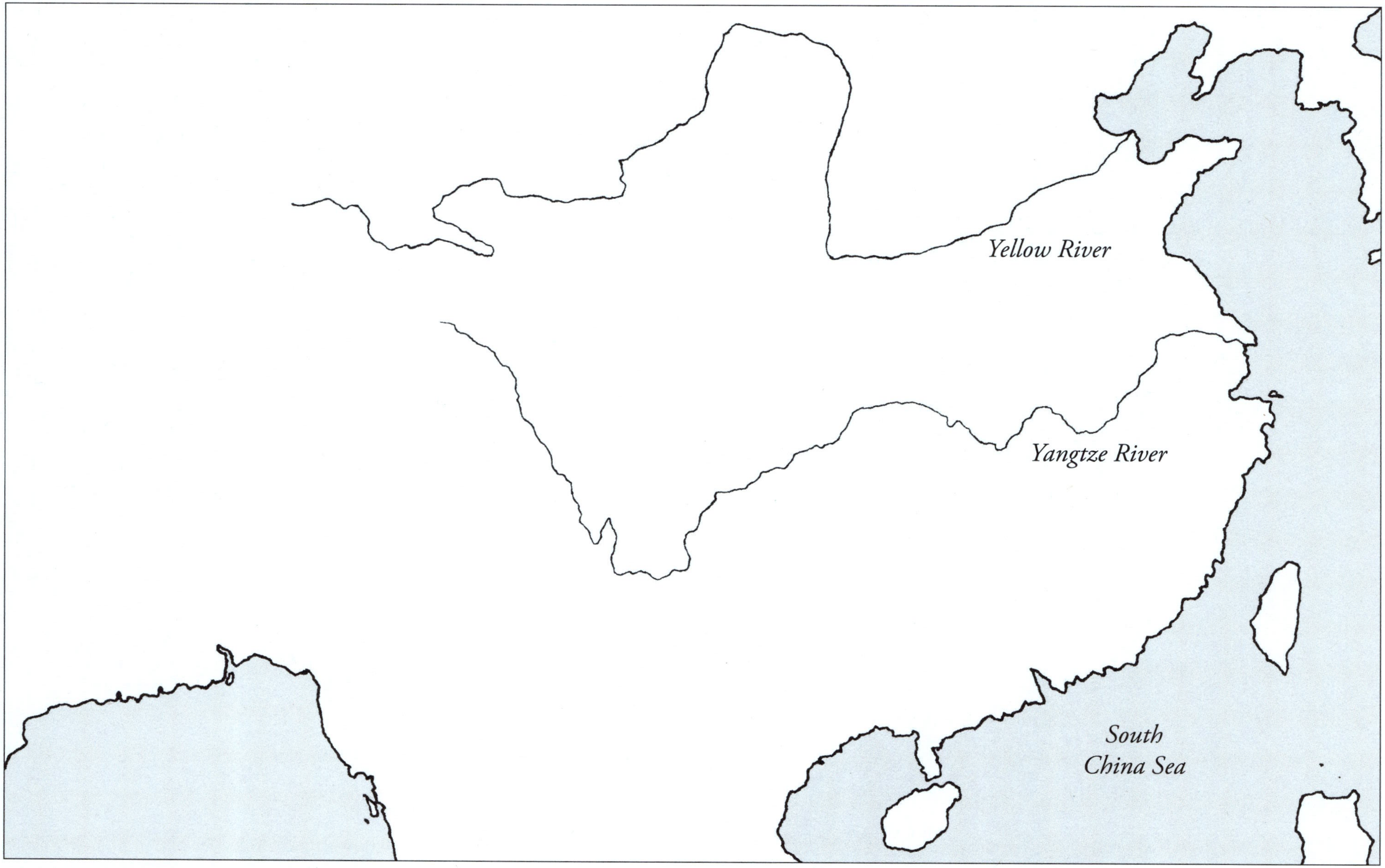

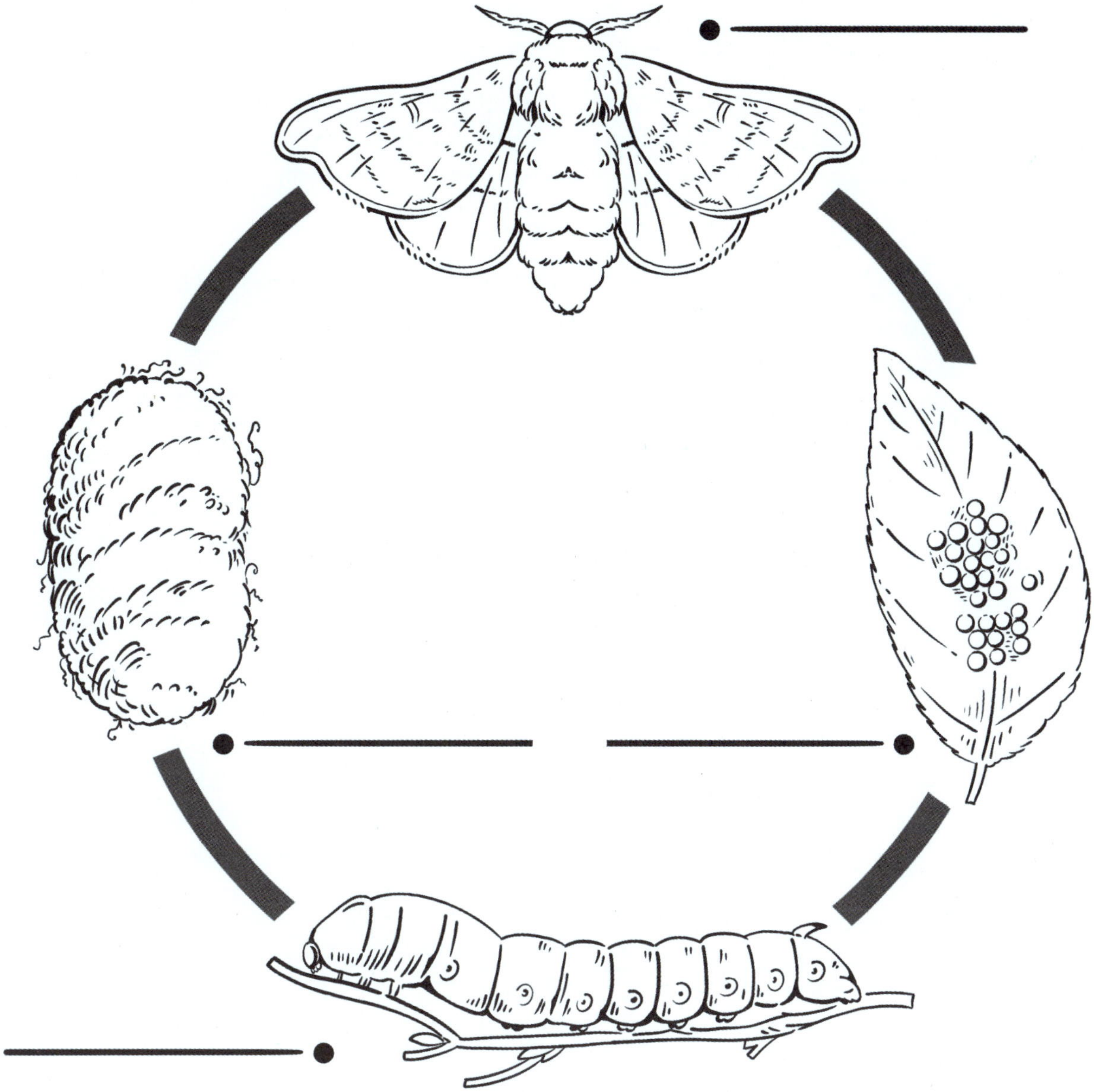

1. EGGS
2. LARVA
3. PUPA
4. ADULT

Name ______________________ Date ____________

Ancient Peoples of West Africa

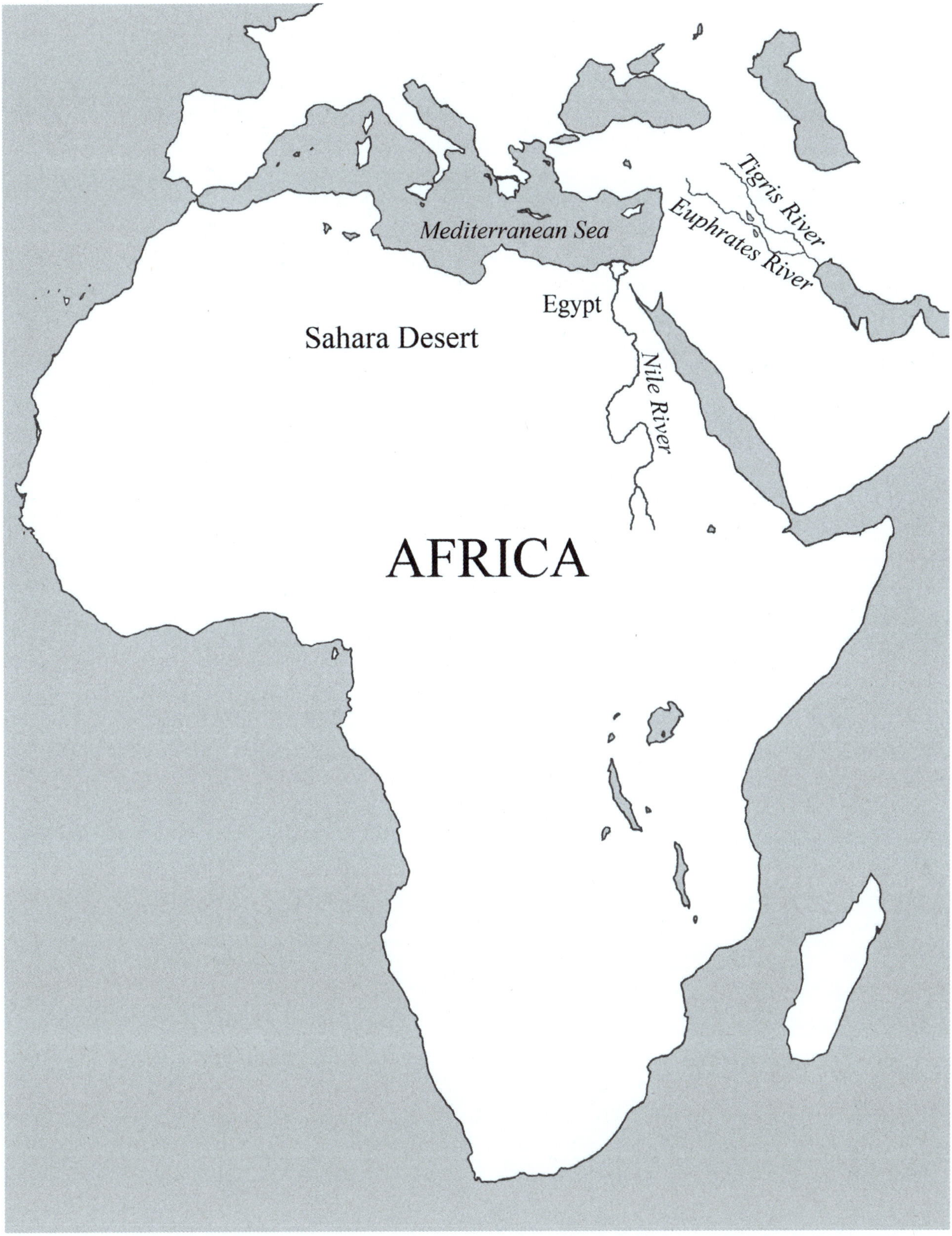

ANANSI AND TURTLE

Name ______________________

Date ______________________

Bull-Jumpers and Sailors

Bull Jumper

The Minotaur's Maze

The Ancient Nubians

Name ______________________ Date ____________

The Hyksos Invade Egypt

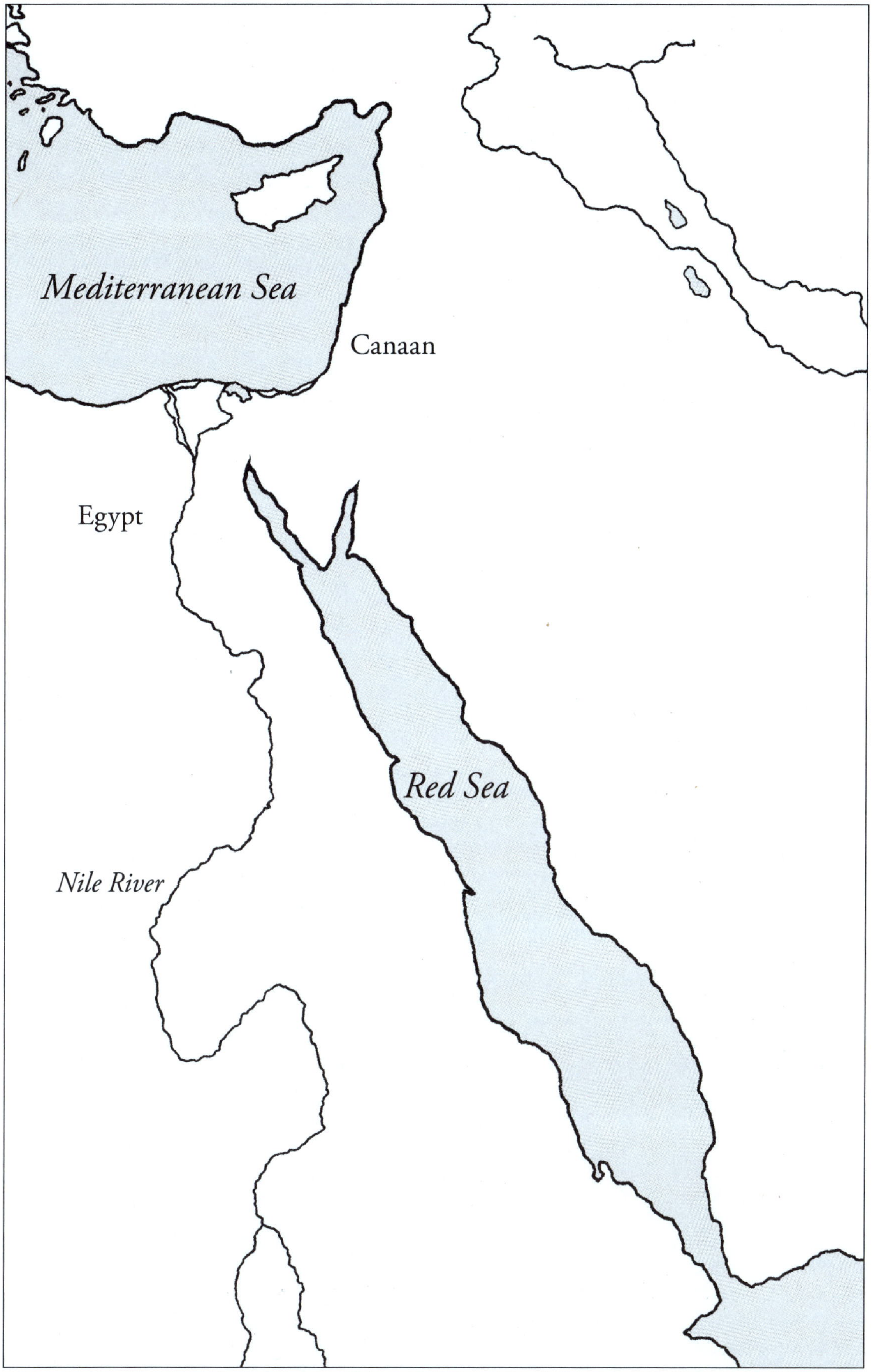

Name ______________________________ Date ____________

Amenhotep and King Tut

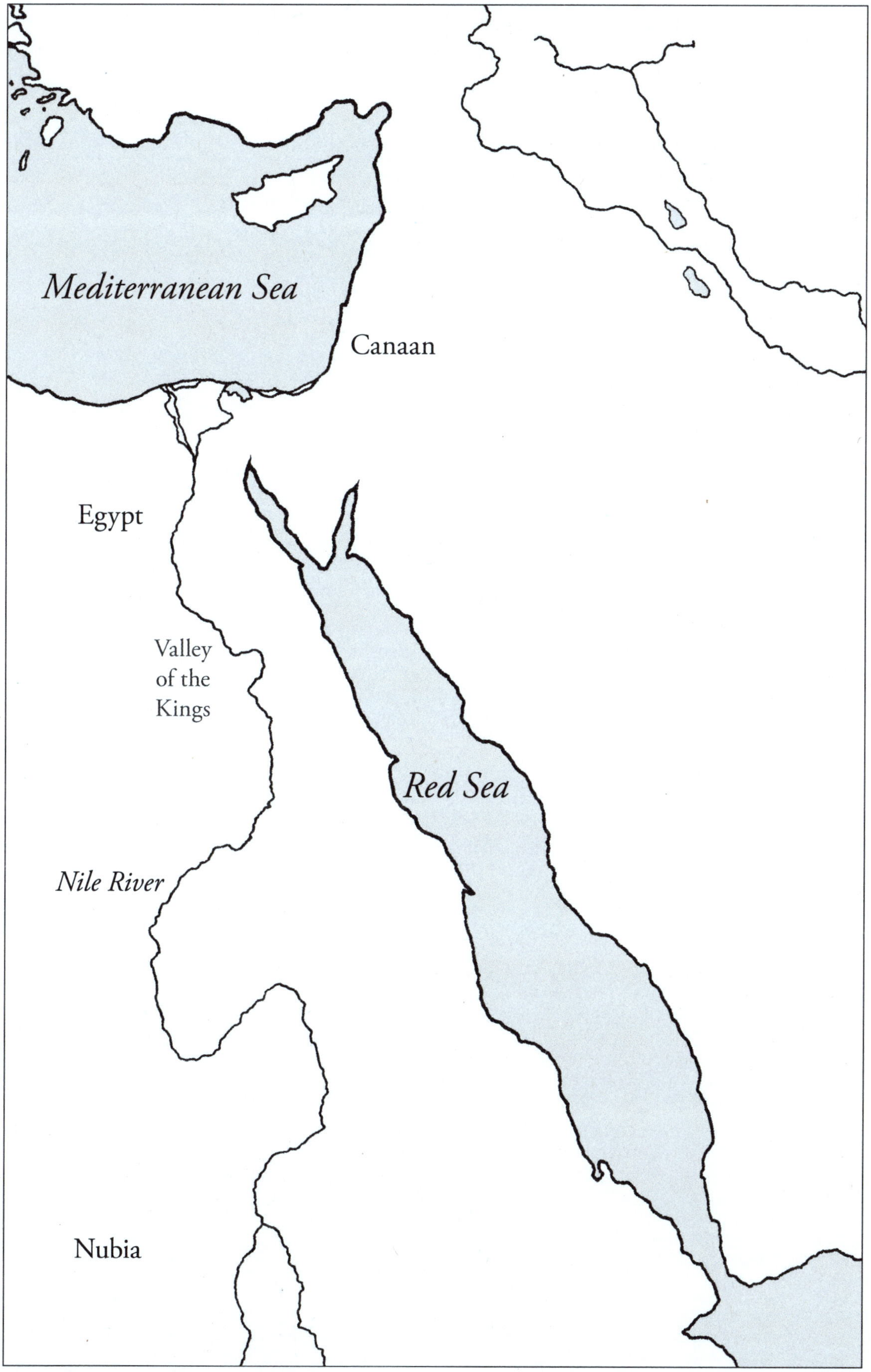

The Mask of King Tut

Name ______________________ Date __________

The Exodus from Egypt

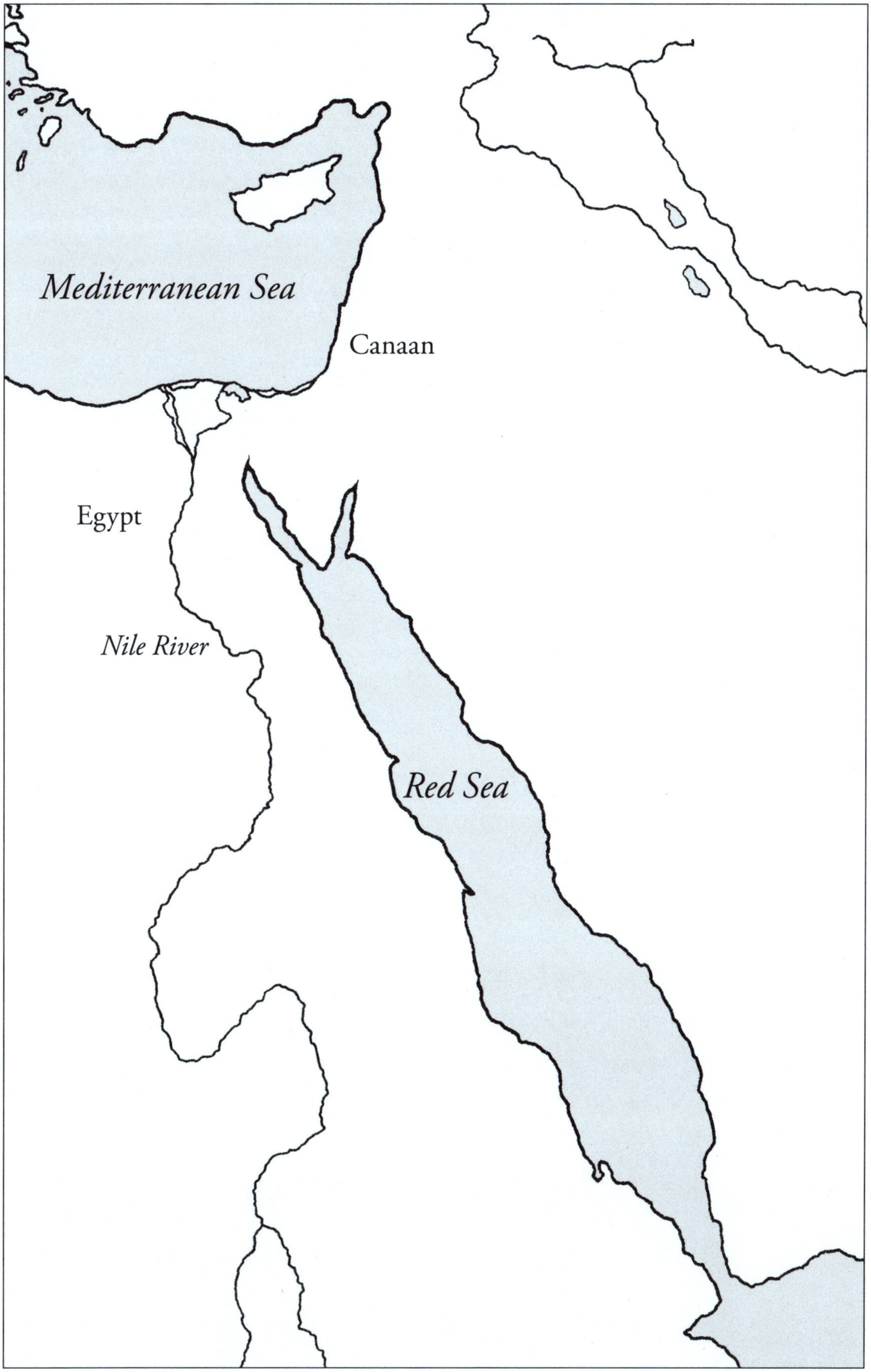

Moses Leads the Israelites Across the Red Sea

Name ______________________

Date ______________________

The Mycenaeans

GREEK WAR CHARIOT

A GREEK VASE

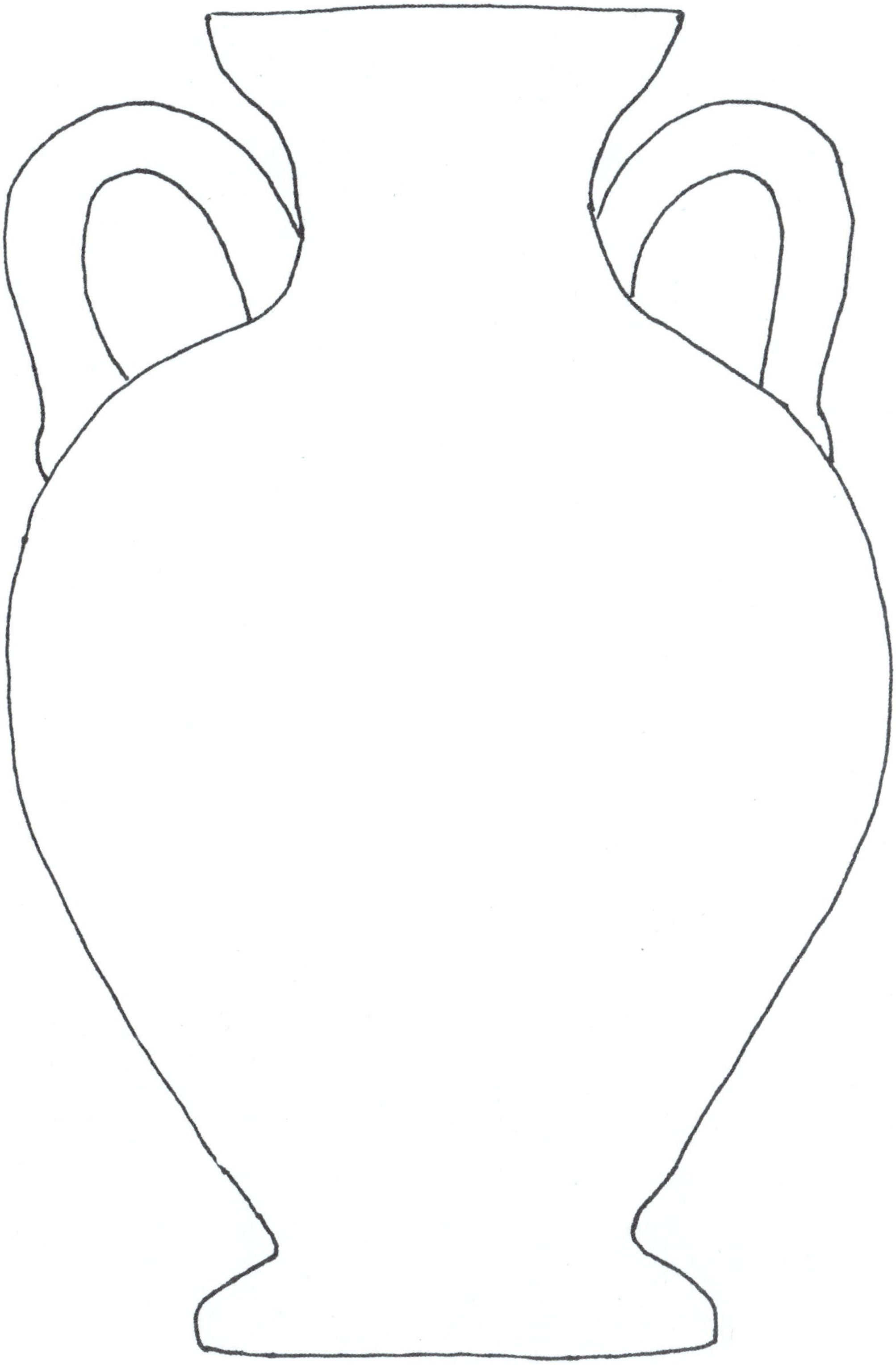

Name ______________________

Date ______________________

Phoenician Traders

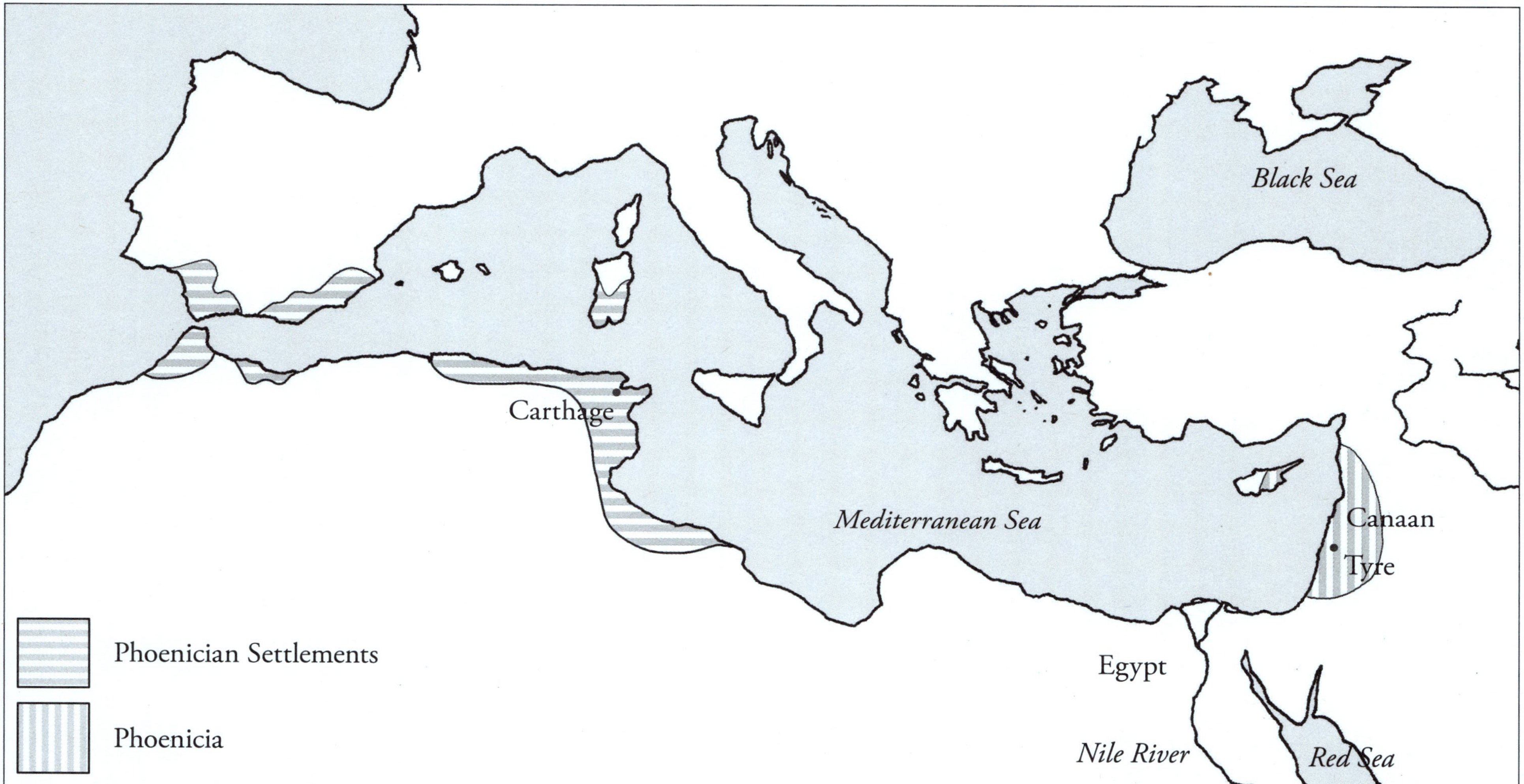

A Phoenician Ship

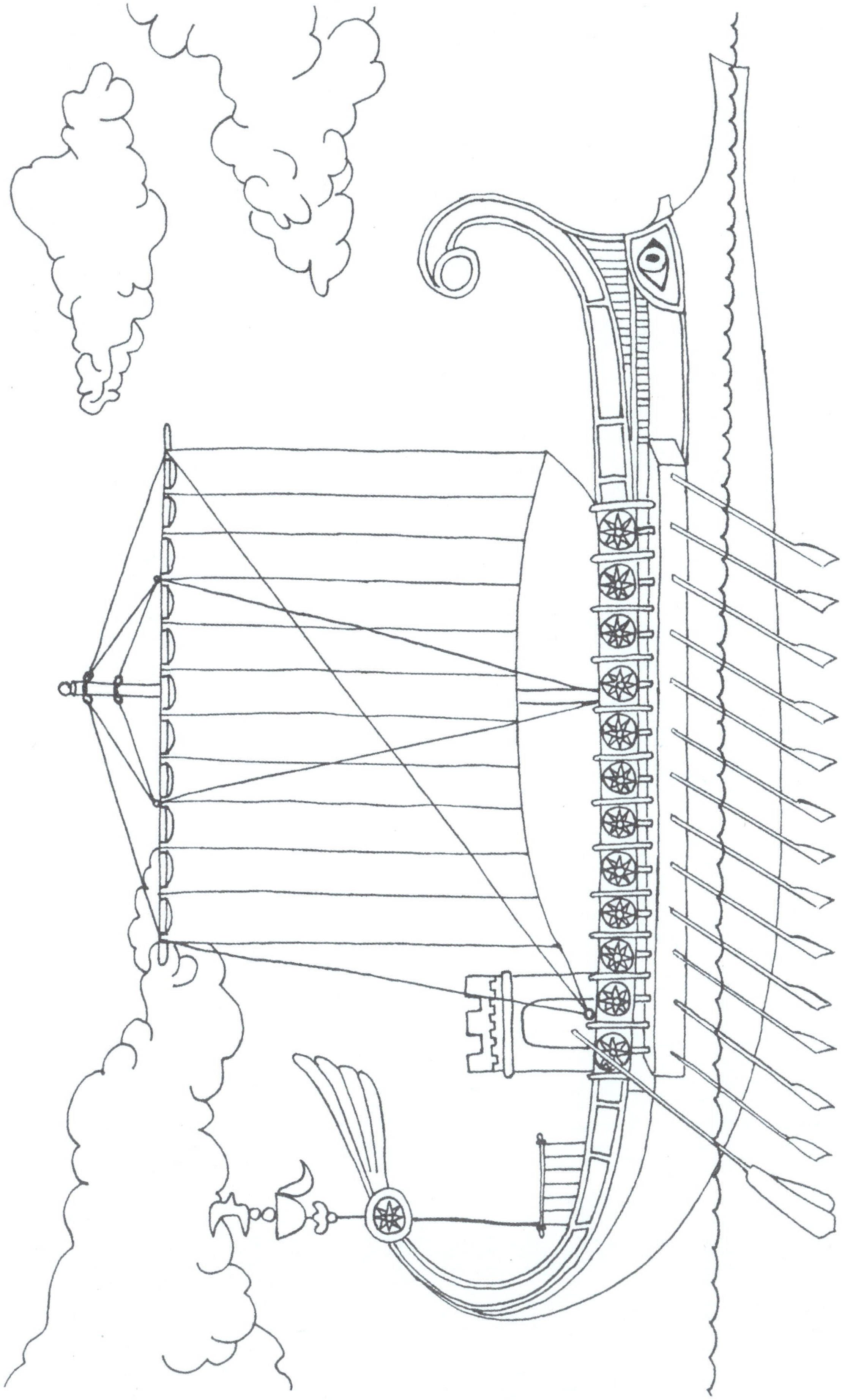

Dido Measures Her Land

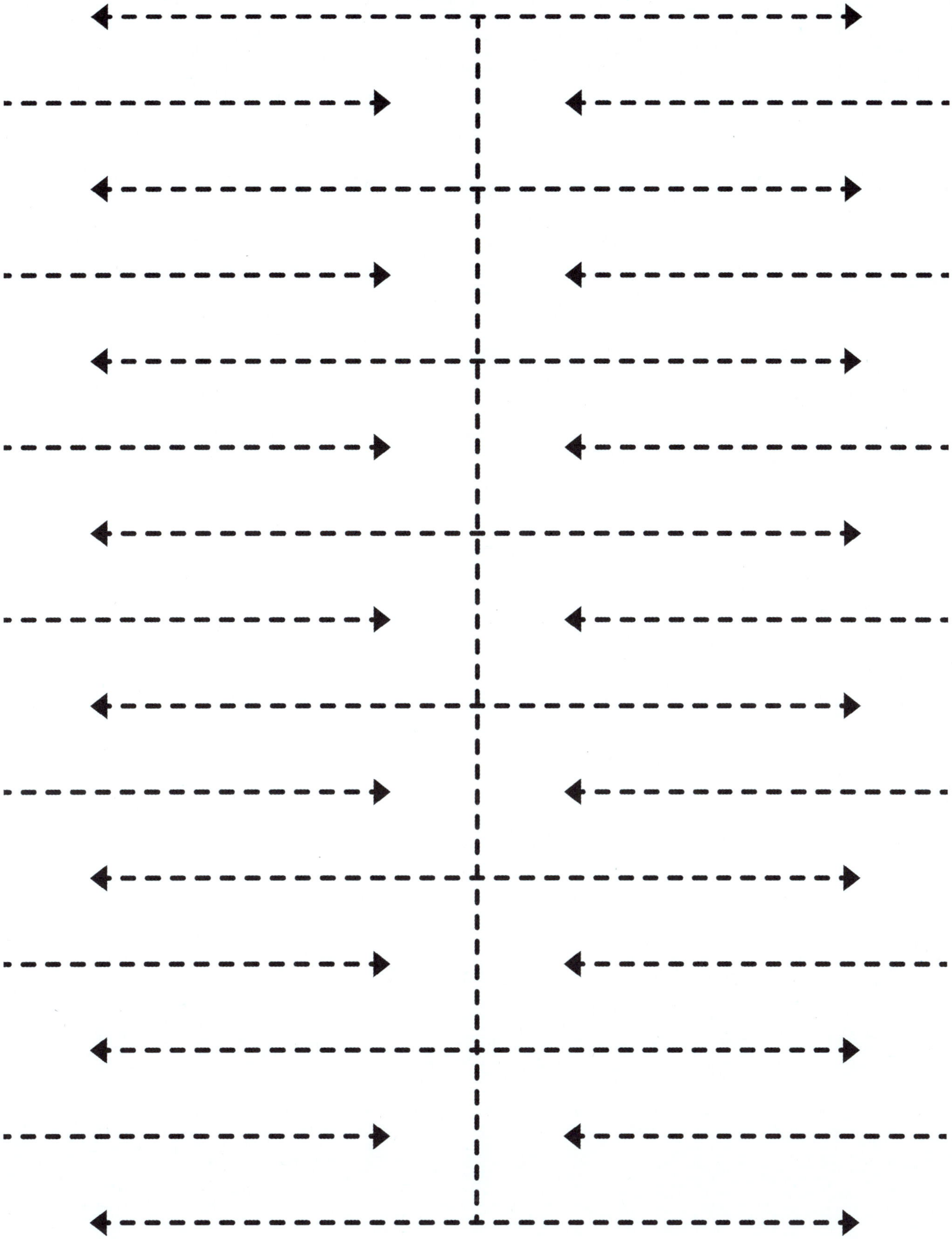

A Bas-Relief From Ancient Assyria

Name ______________________

Date ______________________

The Library of Nineveh

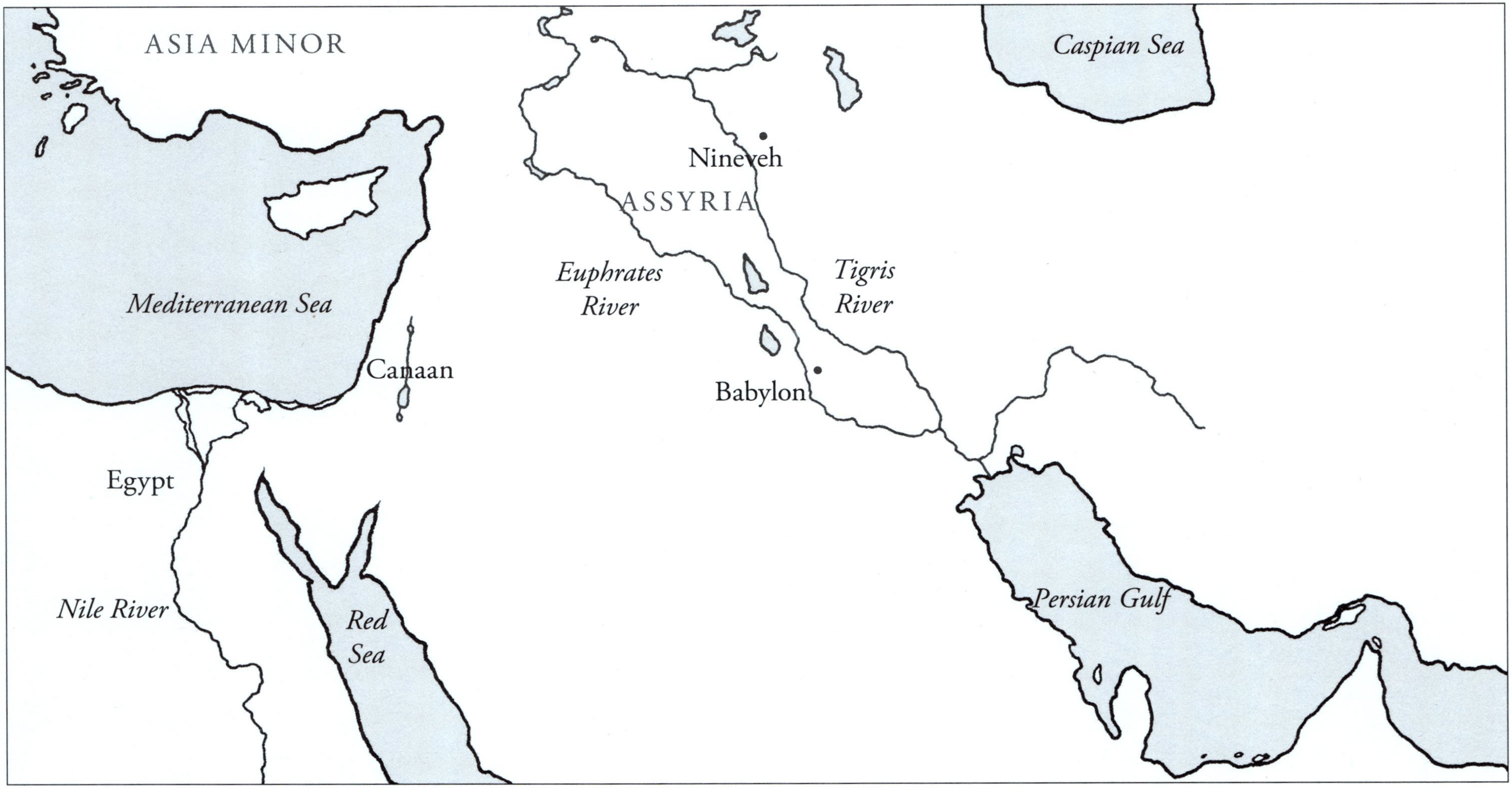

Queen Shammuramat

ALPHA	BETA	GAMMA
DELTA	EPSILON	PI
SIGMA	OMEGA	

Α,α	Β,β	Γ,γ
Δ,δ	Ε,ε	Π,π
Σ,σ	Ω,ω	

Write Your Name with Greek Letters

Using the Greek alphabet to the right, write your name in Greek.

____

____

____

____

English	Capital	Lower-Case
A	Α	α
B	Β	β
G	Γ	γ
D	Δ	δ
E (short)	Ε	ε
Z	Ζ	ζ
E (long)	Η	η
Th	Θ	θ
I	Ι	ι
K	Κ	κ
L	Λ	λ
M	Μ	μ
N	Ν	ν
CH	Ξ	ξ
O (short)	Ο	ο
P	Π	π
R	Ρ	ρ
S	Σ	σ
T	Τ	τ
U	Υ	υ
Ph	Φ	φ
X	Χ	χ
PS	Ψ	ψ
O (long)	Ω	ω

Name ______________________

Date ______________________

The Stories of Homer

The Cyclops

A Spartan Warrior

Greek Paper Dolls

Greek Paper Dolls

outfits

Greek Paper Dolls

outfit and accessories

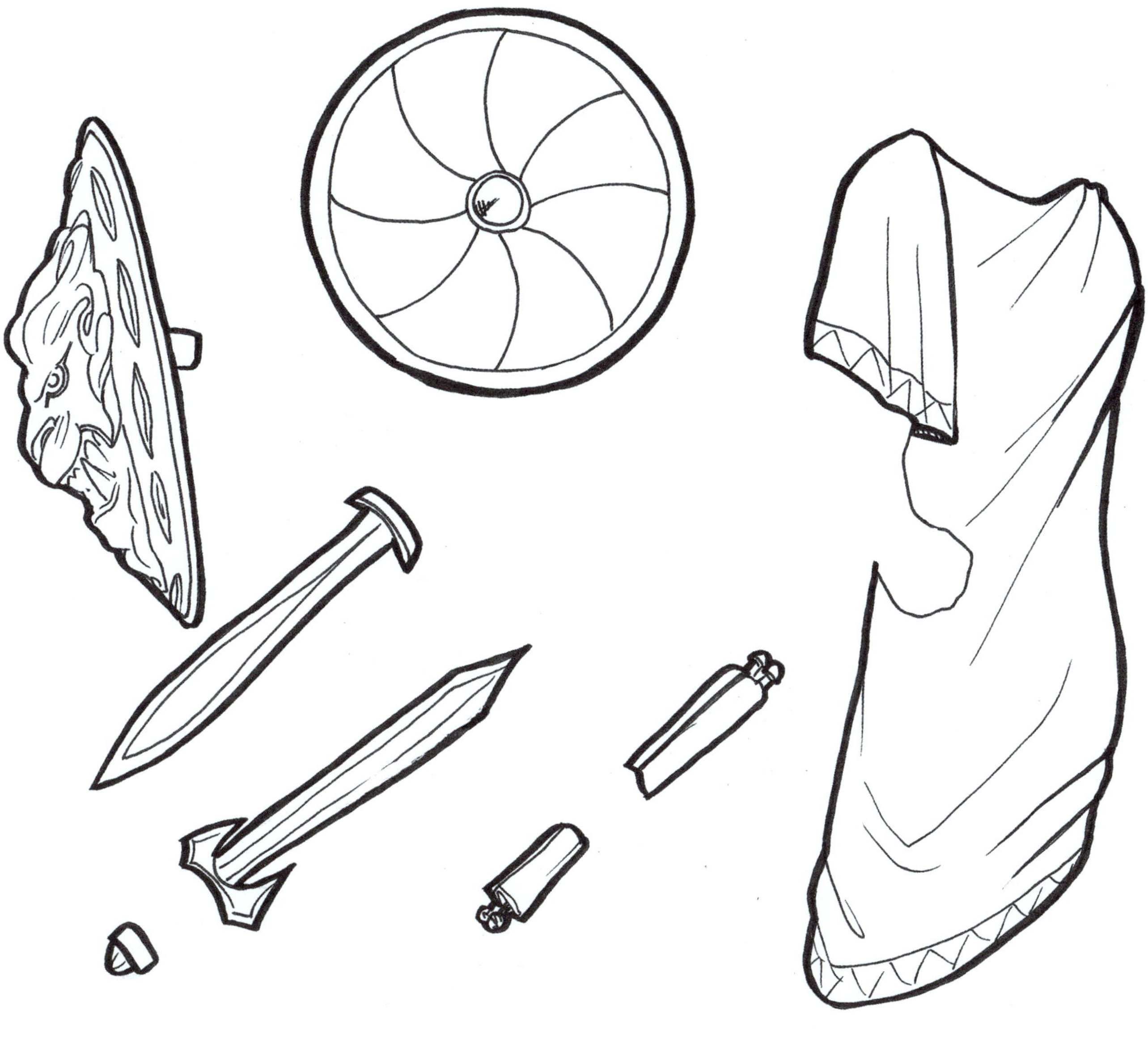

Name ________________________________ Date ______________

Athens and Sparta

Draco Flees Athens

Name ______

Date ______

Ancient Greece

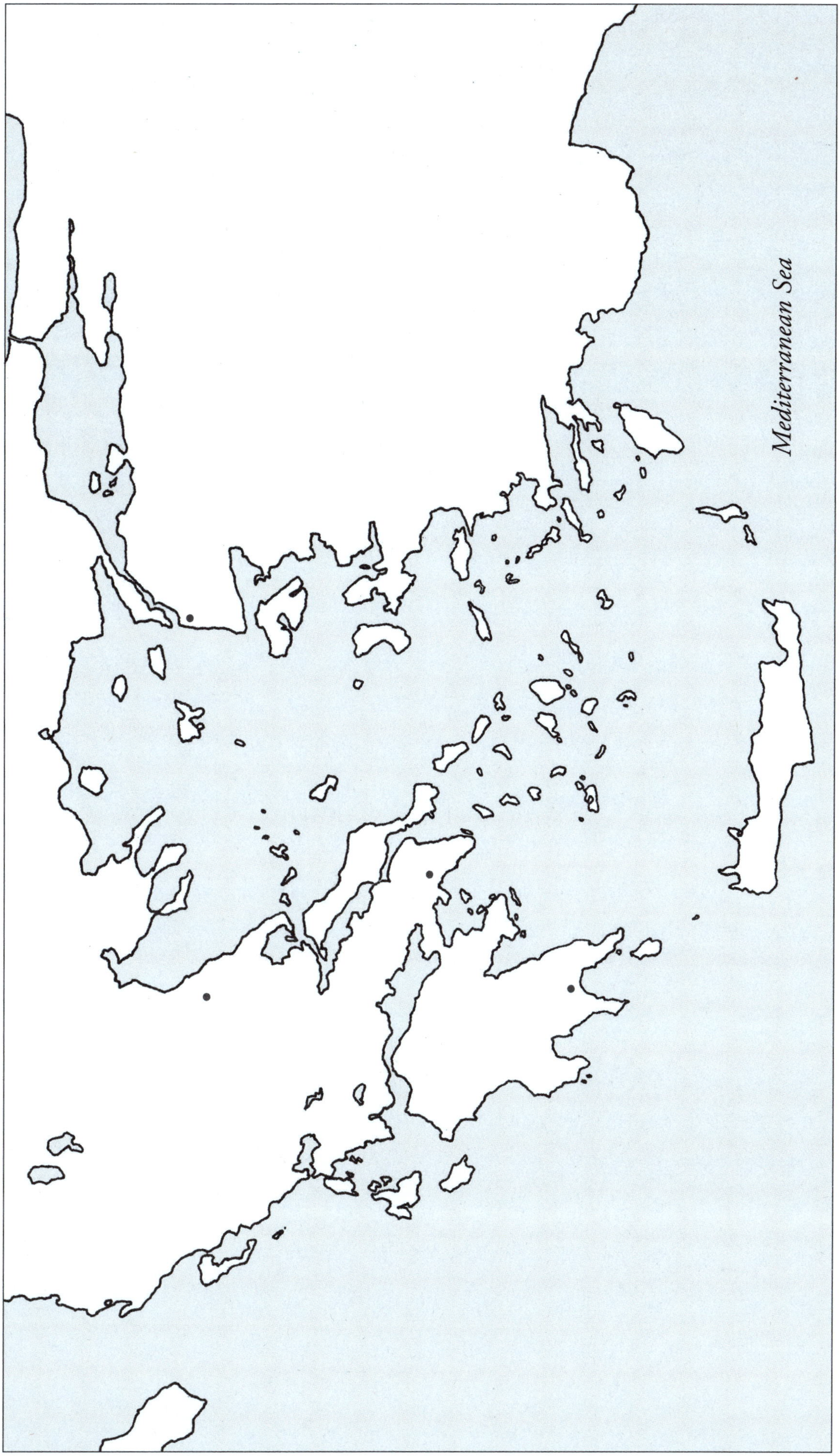

Athena and Zeus

Greek Gods and Goddesses Word Search

Find these words from the story of the Golden Apple in the word search below. Words are only across or down.

Mount Olympus	Aphrodite	Eris	Athena
Greece	Paris	Zeus	Troy
Hera	Beautiful	Apple	Helen

G	S	P	A	P	H	R	O	D	I	T	E
R	Z	I	P	F	E	Q	L	O	O	K	X
E	A	H	P	G	O	T	W	G	H	Z	A
E	U	W	L	Z	E	R	I	S	E	E	T
C	S	M	E	B	V	O	X	I	L	Y	H
E	X	J	R	E	D	Y	P	N	E	M	E
Y	K	I	Z	A	P	L	J	G	N	O	N
B	J	M	S	U	T	S	U	N	R	M	A
M	O	U	N	T	O	L	Y	M	P	U	S
B	P	T	E	I	Y	C	T	O	Y	S	C
O	W	P	J	F	P	A	R	I	S	I	F
Y	O	U	R	U	Z	Q	M	X	B	T	G
H	E	R	A	L	O	N	G	Z	E	U	S

ZEUS

King of gods

POSEIDON

God of the sea

HERA

Queen of the gods, wife of Zeus

DEMETER

Goddess of the harvest

HESTIA

Goddess of the hearth and fire

APHRODITE

Goddess of love and beauty

ATHENA

Goddess of wisdom and warfare

ARTEMIS

Goddess of the hunt, wilderness, and childbirth

APOLLO

God of the sun, music, and poetry

ARES

God of war

HERMES

Messenger of the gods, god of trade

HEPHAESTUS

God of fire, metalworking, and sculpture

ROMULUS *and* REMUS

Name ____________________

Date ____________________

The Power of Rome

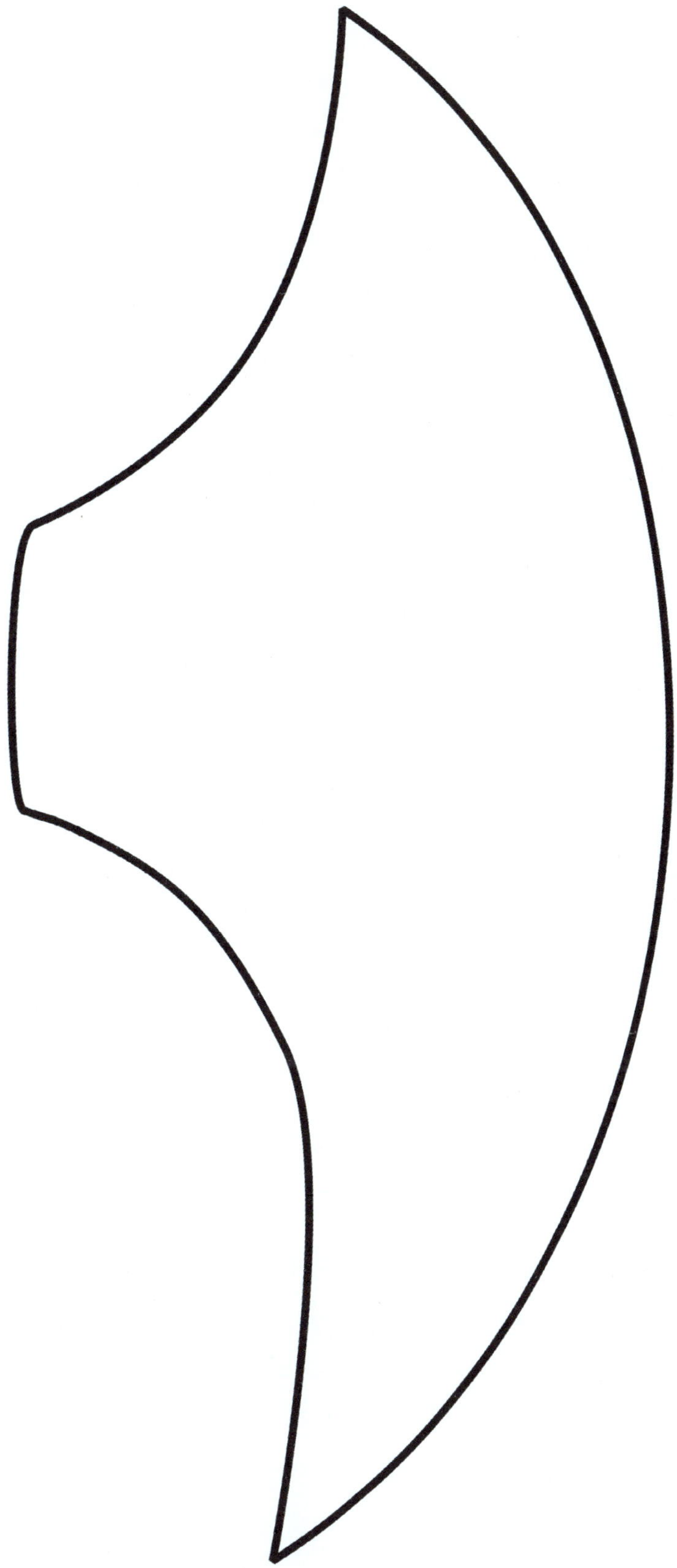

The King and Queen of Rome

Name ______________________

Date ______________________

Nebuchadnezzar’s Madness

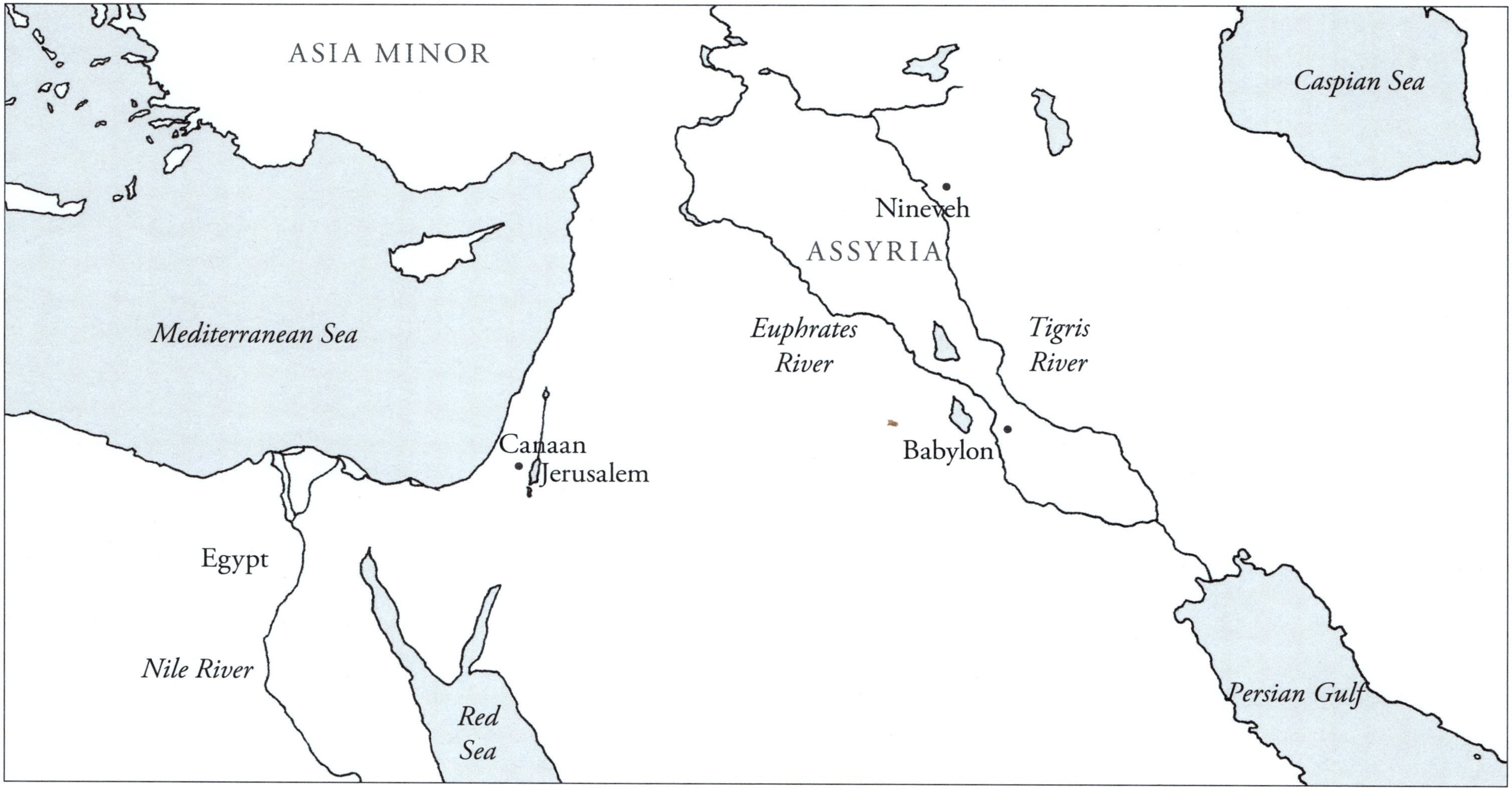

The Ishtar Gate

Marduk and Tiamat

THE TEMPLE OF ARTEMIS AT EPHESUS
(Greek colony)

THE GREAT PYRAMID OF GIZA
(Egypt)

THE HANGING GARDENS OF BABYLON
(Babylon)

THE STATUE OF ZEUS AT OLYMPIA
(Greece)

THE MAUSOLEUM AT HALICARNASSUS
(Persian Empire)

THE COLOSSUS OF RHODES
(Greece)

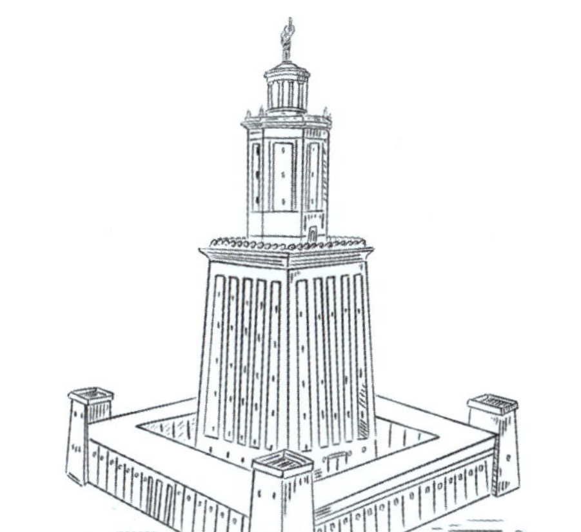

THE LIGHTHOUSE OF ALEXANDRIA
(Egypt)

Name ____________________

Date ____________________

A New Empire

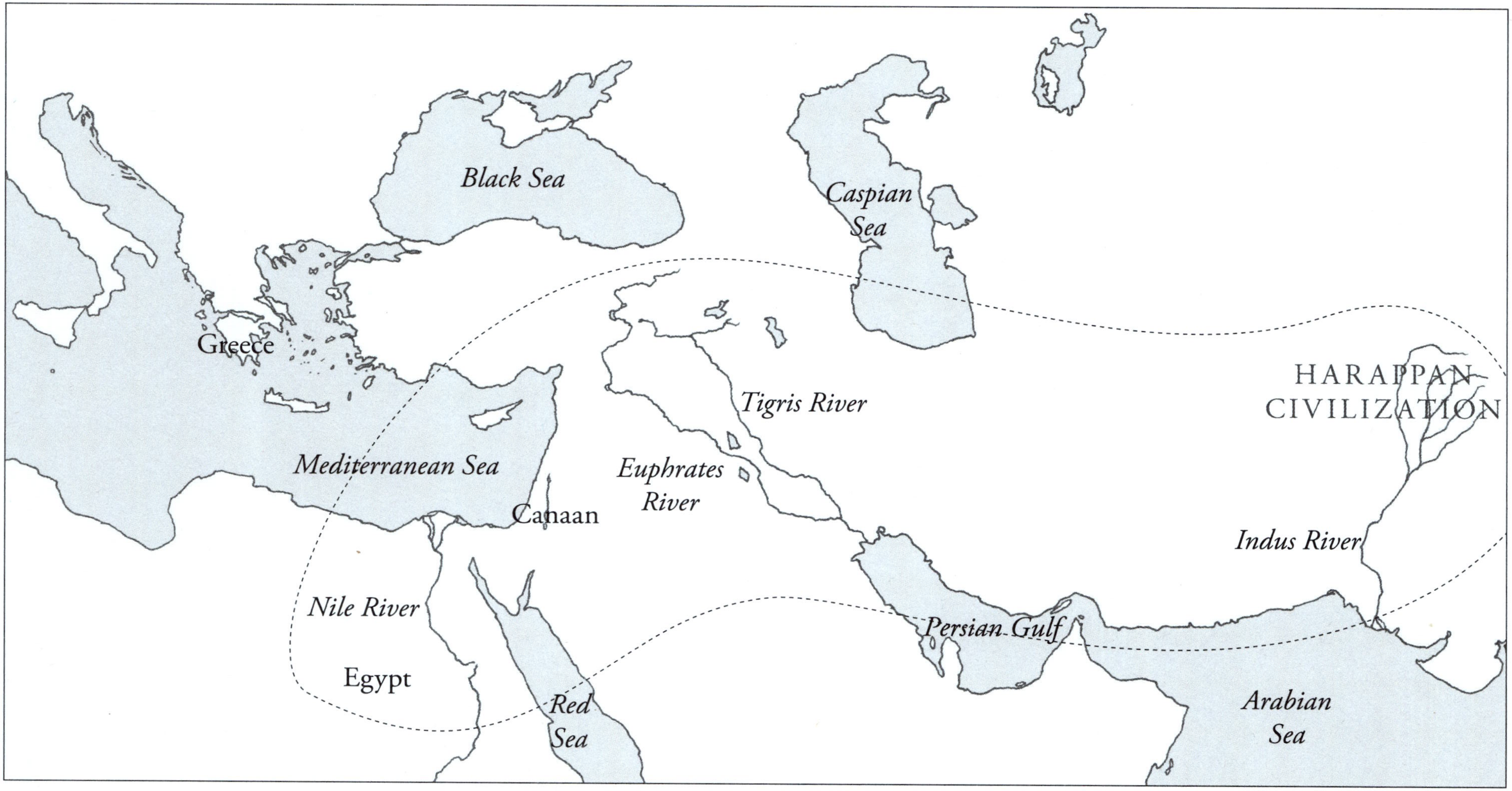

Cyrus the Great

MESOPOTAMIAN CONQUEST!

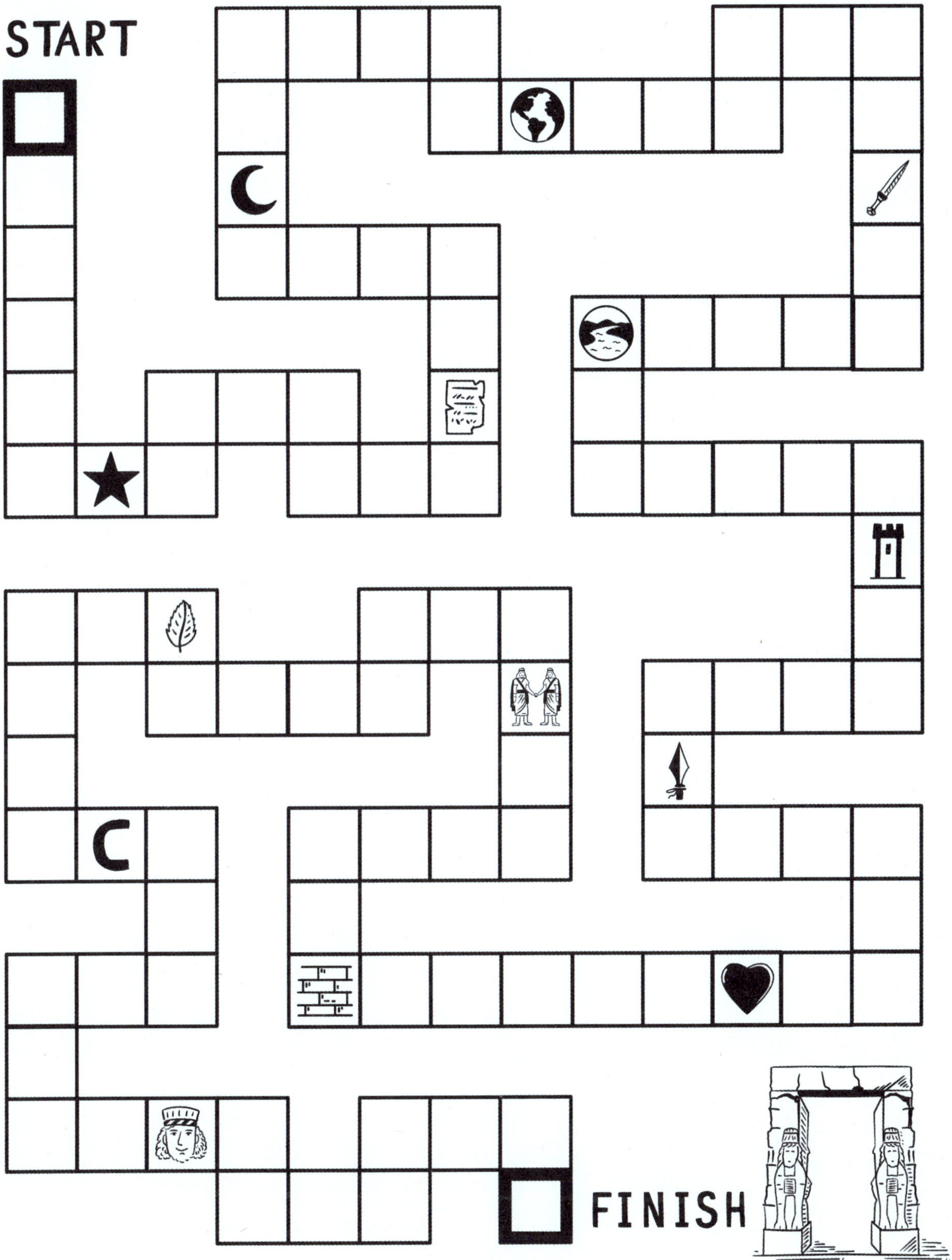

Name ______________________________ Date ____________

Life on the Ganges River

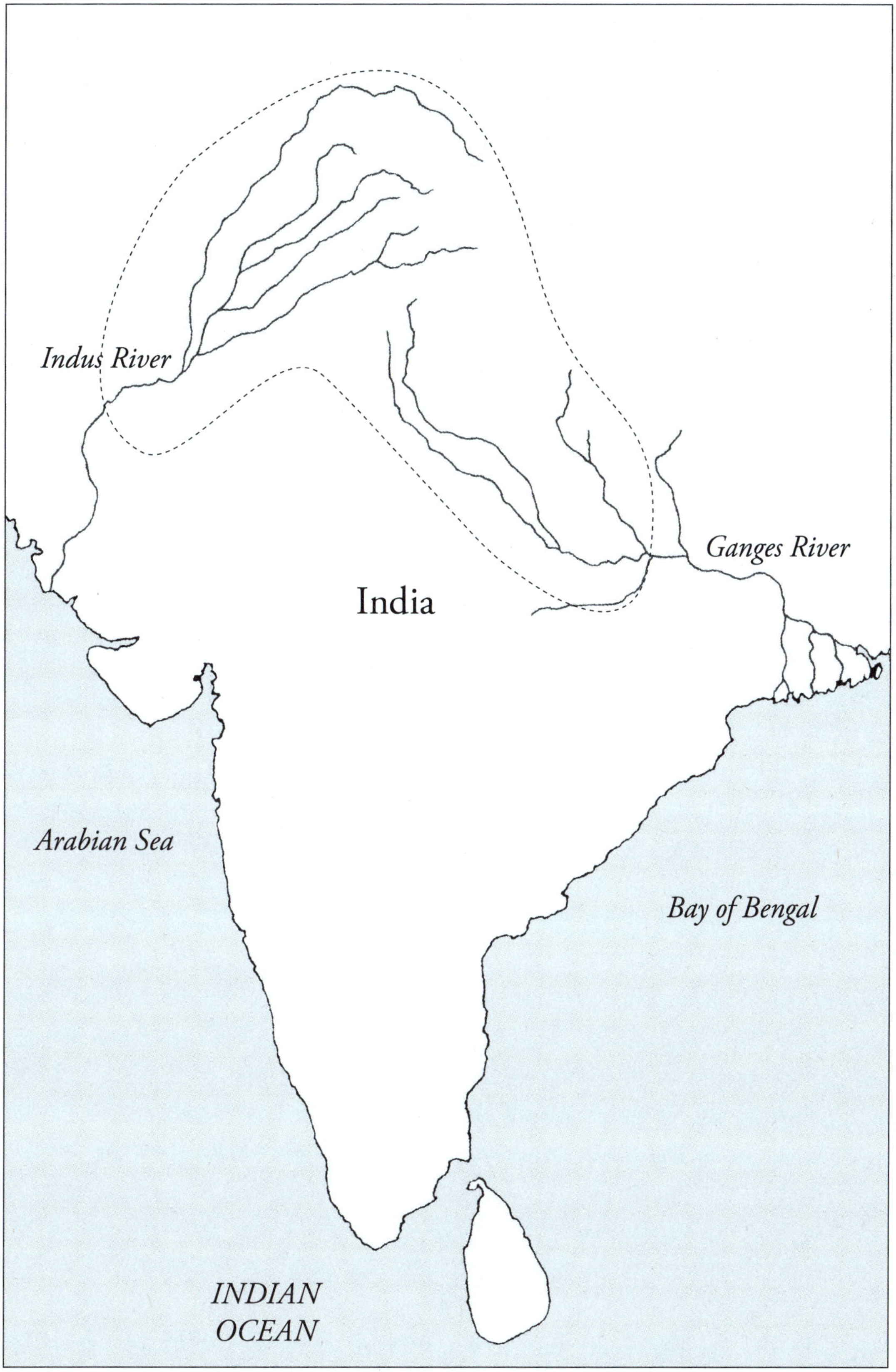

Ajatashatru Travels to Meet the Buddha

Name ____________________

Date ____________________

Confucius: China's Wise Teacher

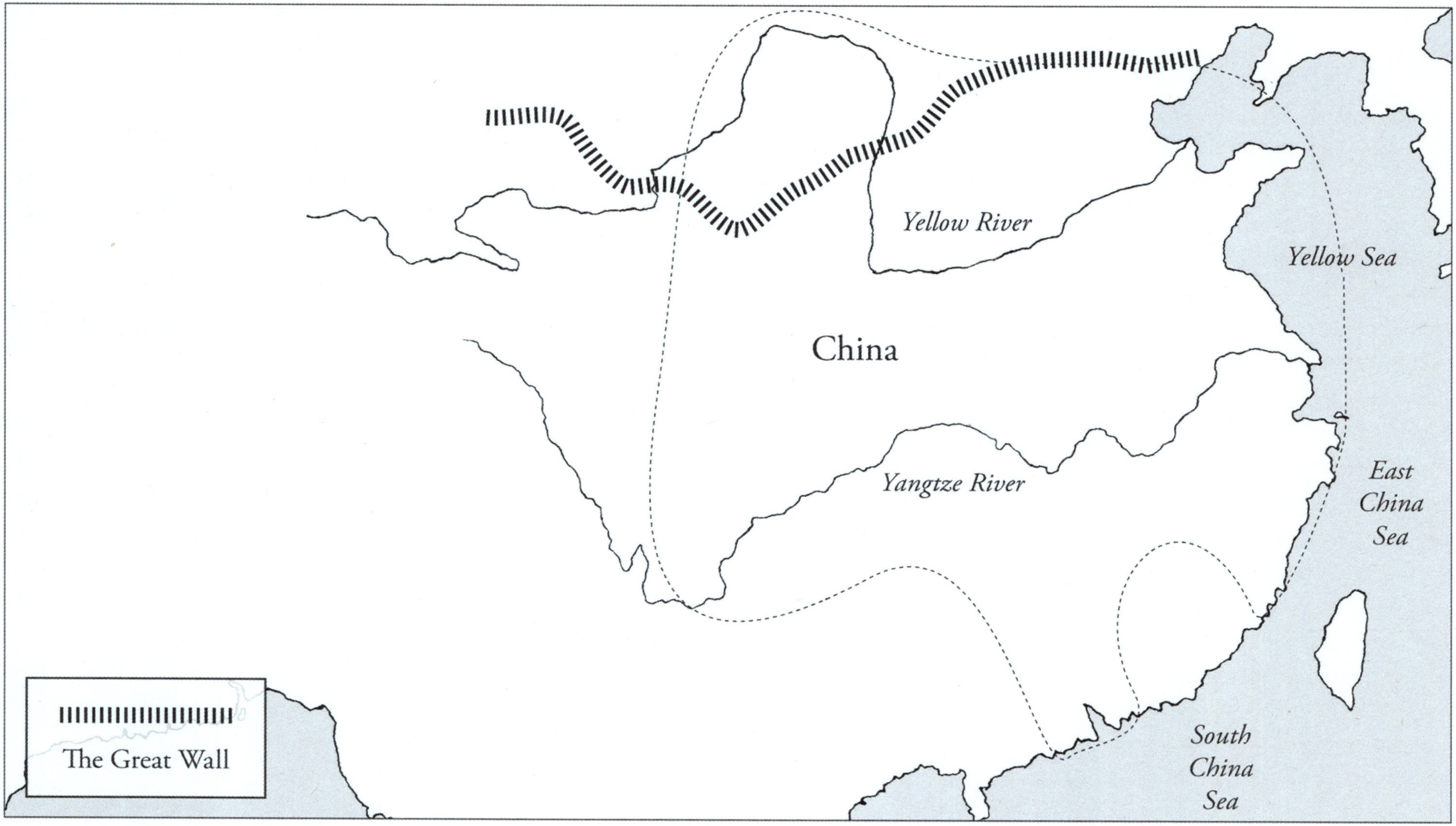

Confucius
China's Wise Teacher

Mencius

Name ______________________

Date ______________________

Greece's War with Persia

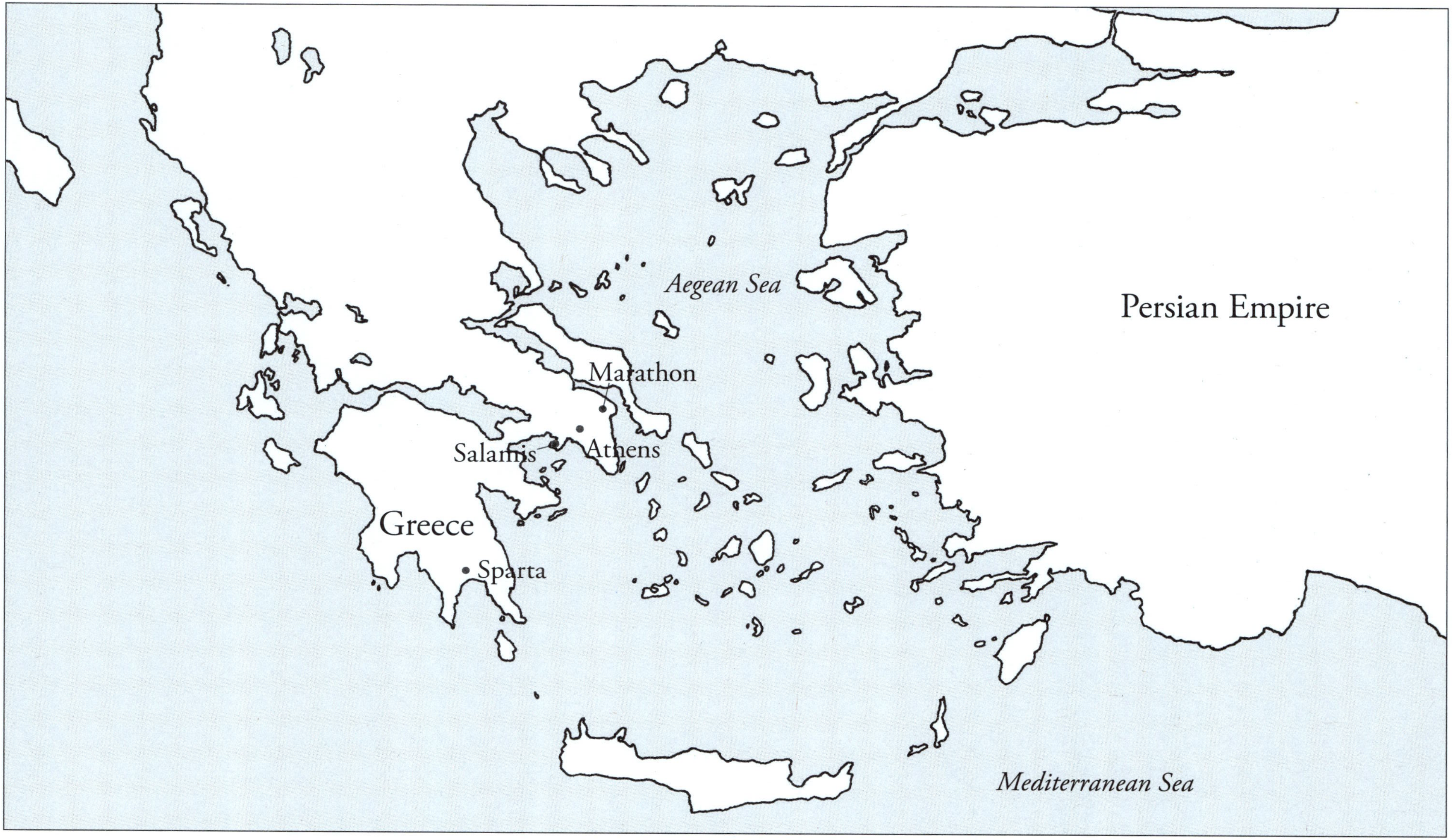

RUN A MARATHON!

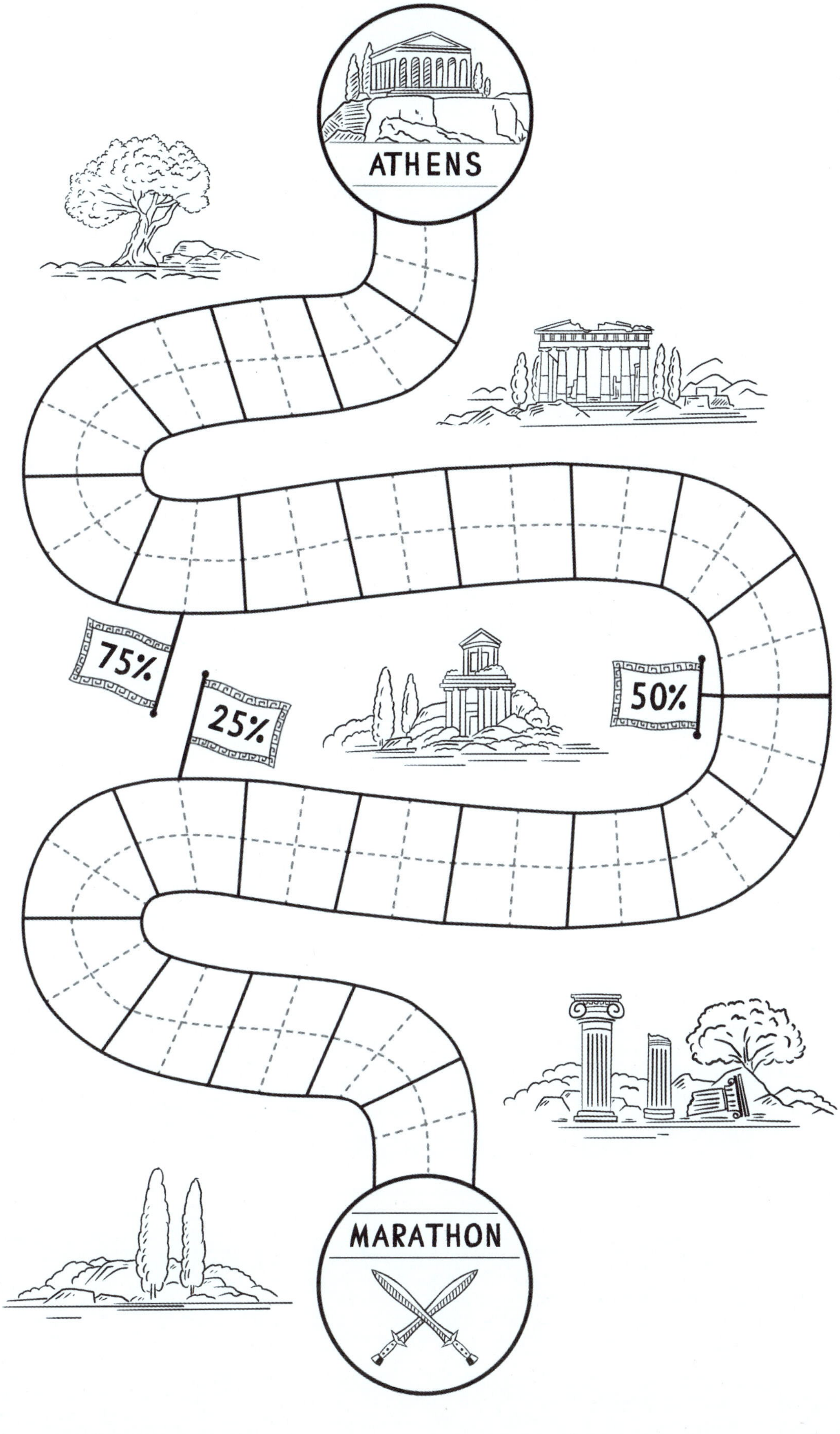

THE PARTHENON

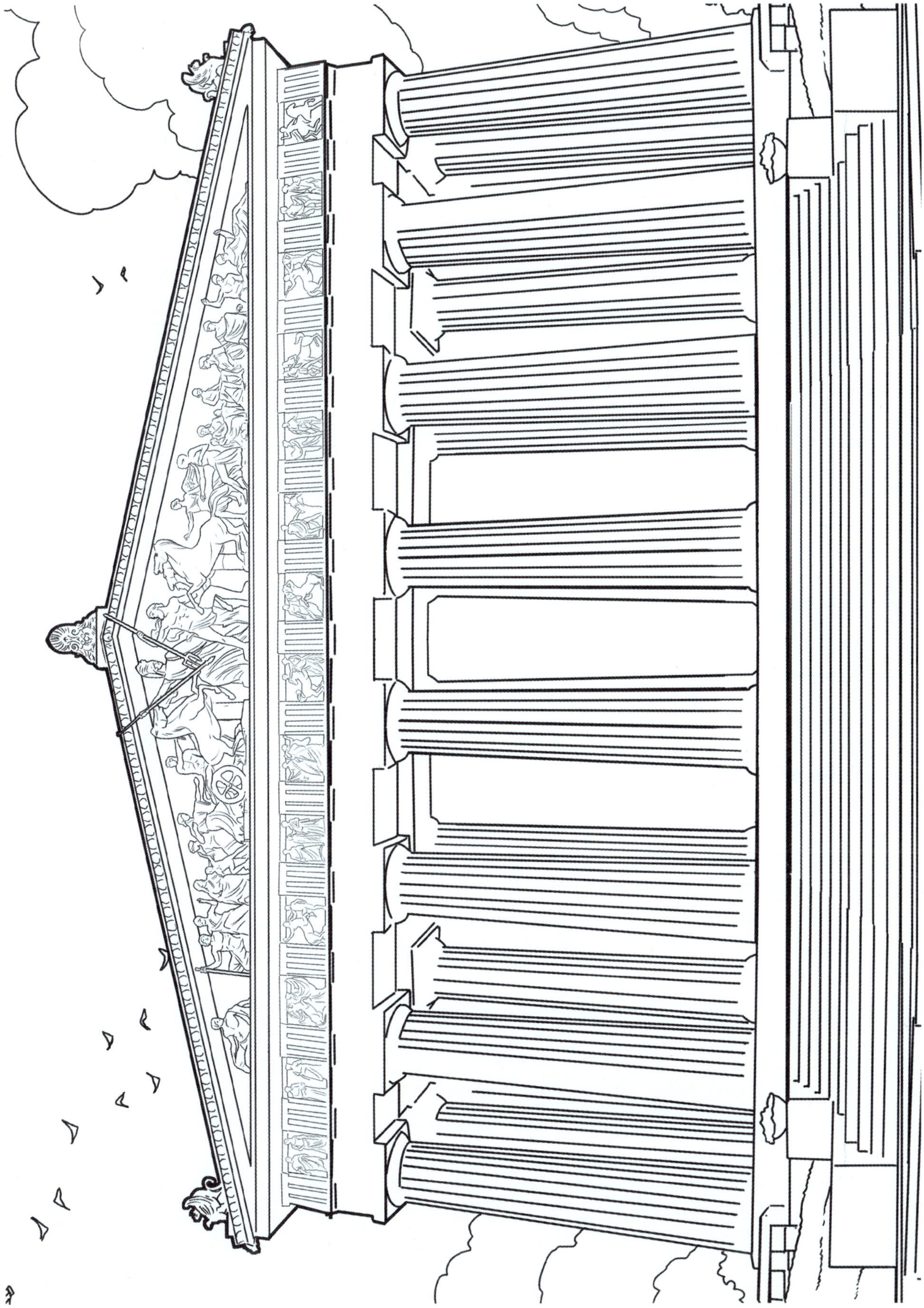

DORIC

IONIC

CORINTHIAN

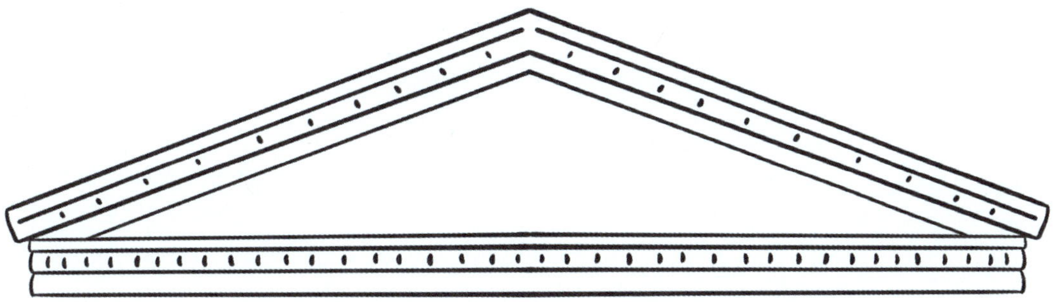

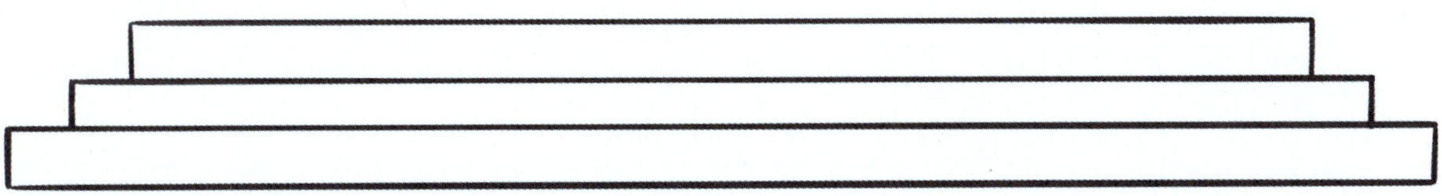

Alexander the Great and Bucephalus

Tie a Gordian Knot

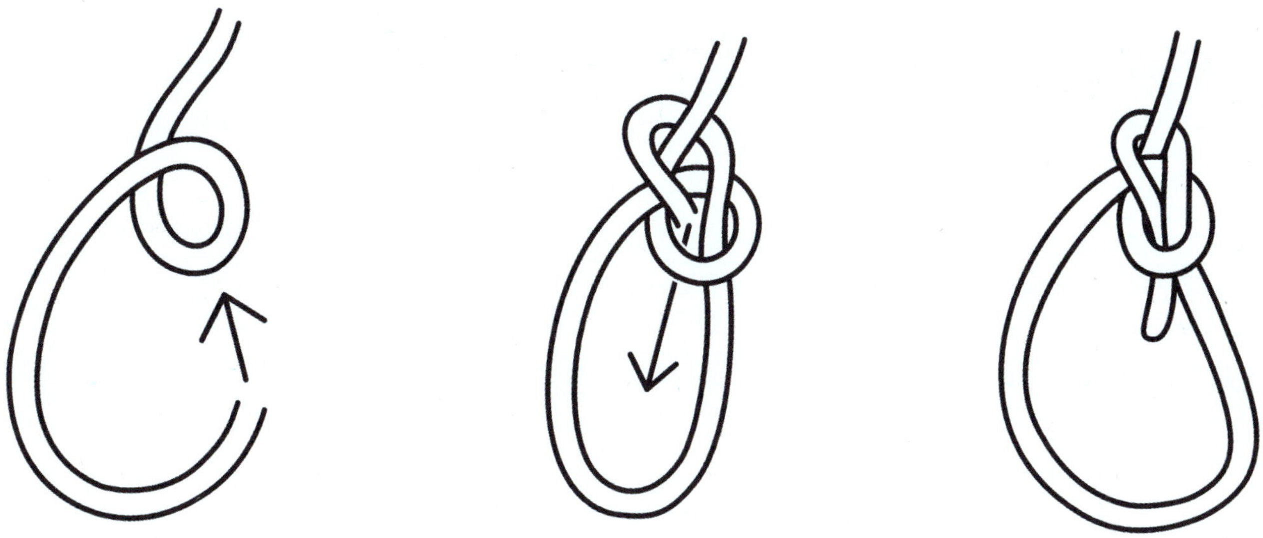

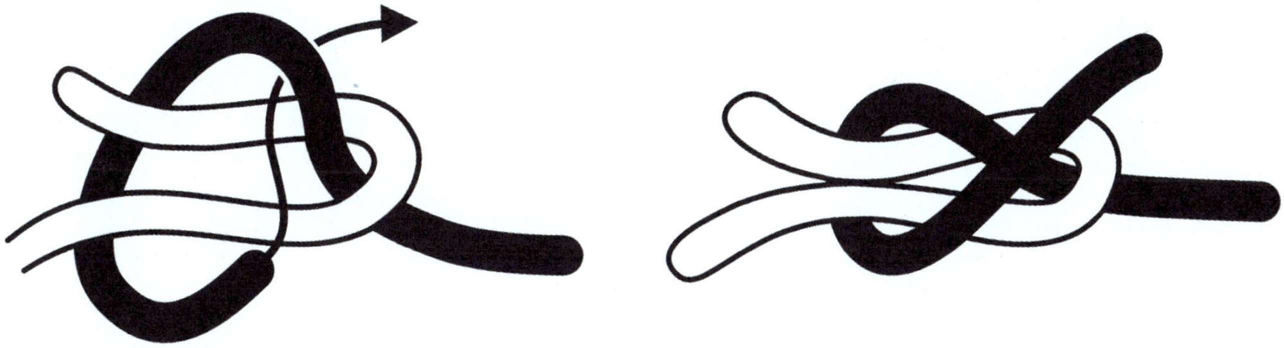

Name ______________________

Date ______________________

Alexander's Invasions

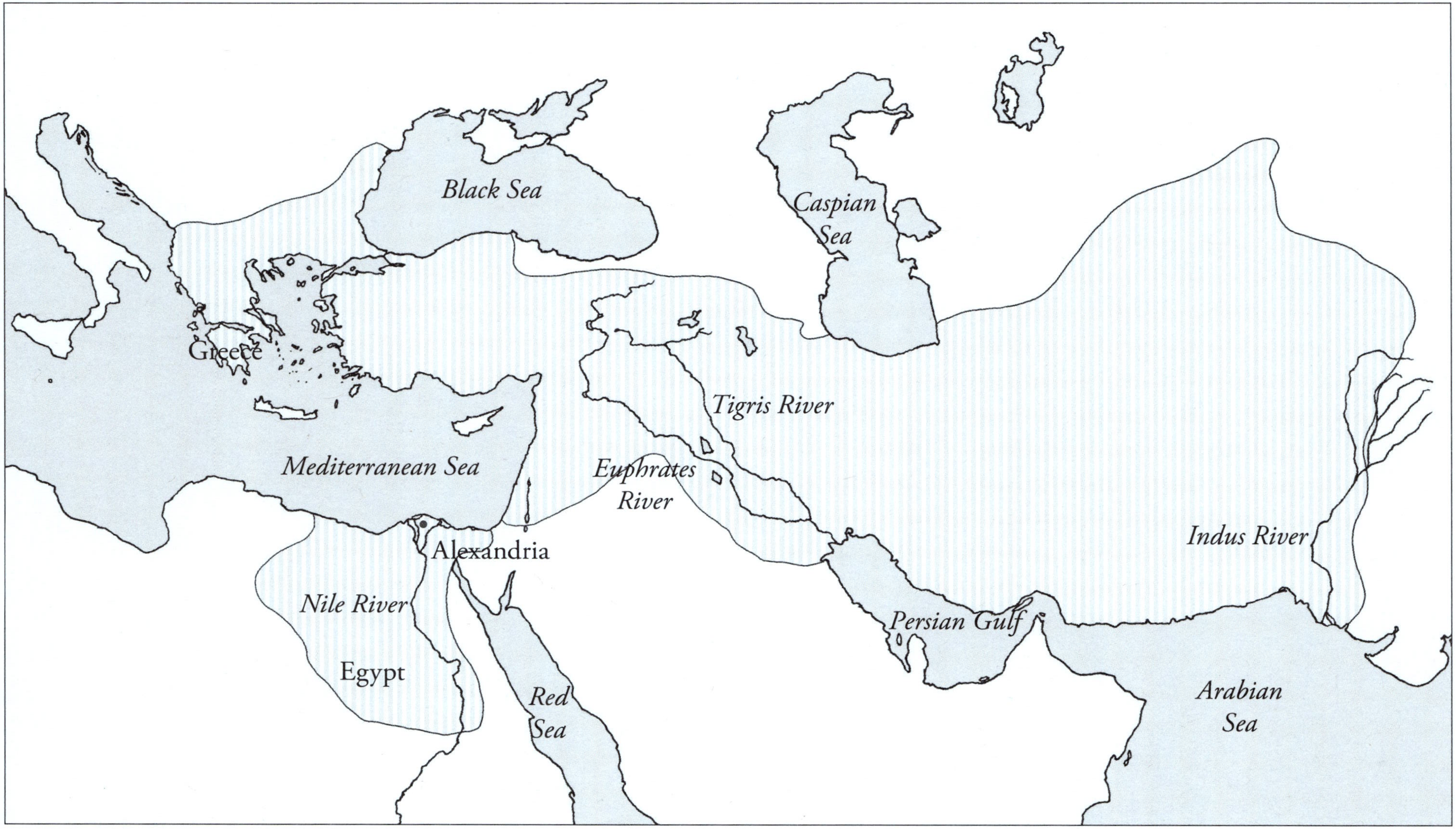

Name ______________________________ Date ____________

The Mauryan Empire

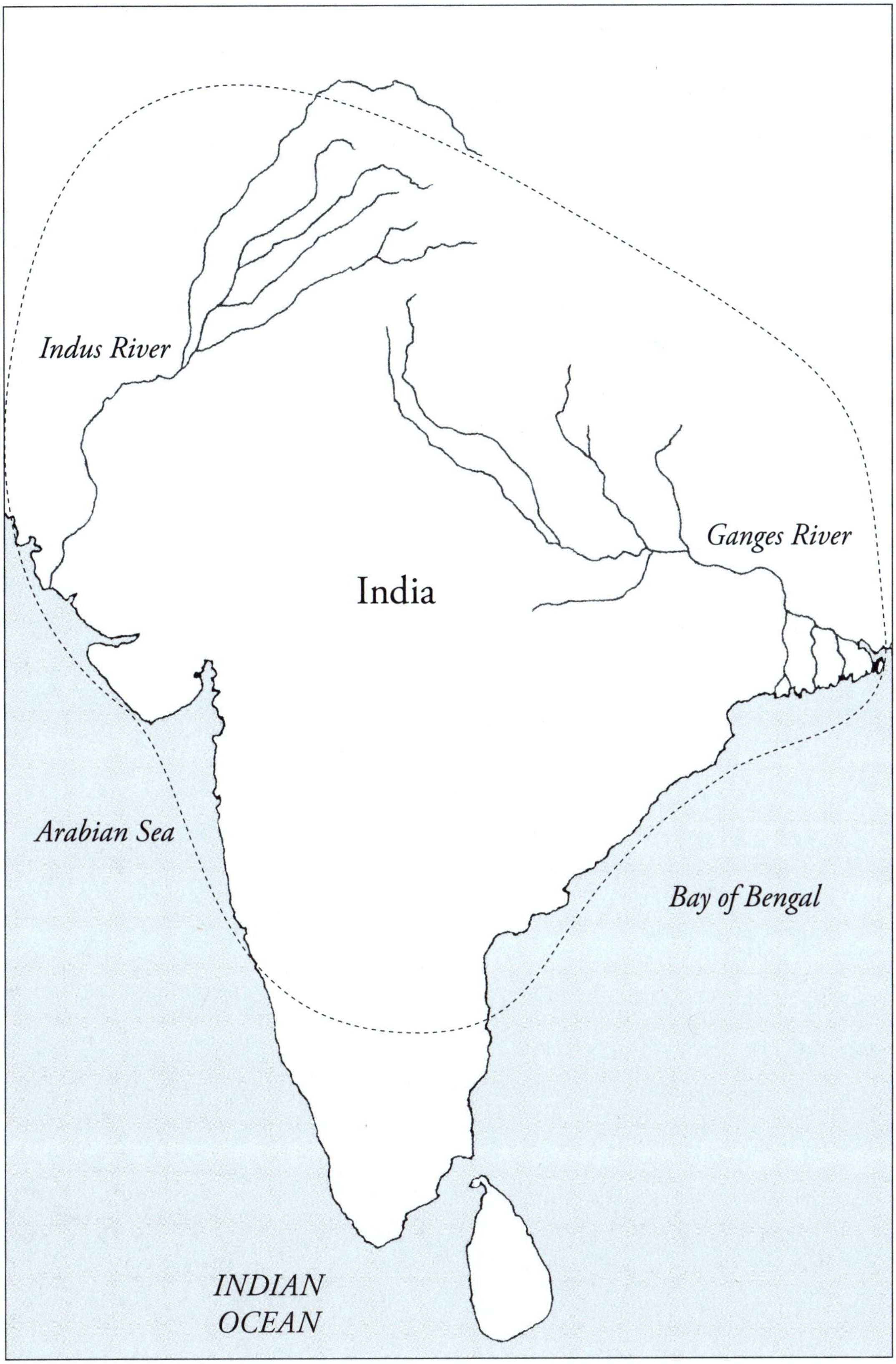

The Jataka Tales

Name ______________________________ Date ____________

Rabbit Shoots the Sun

Rabbit Shoots the Sun

Aqueduct Template

ZEUS
King of gods
JUPITER

POSEIDON
God of the sea
NEPTUNE

HERA
Queen of the gods, wife of Zeus
JUNO

DEMETER
Goddess of the harvest
CERES

HESTIA
Goddess of the hearth and fire
VESTA

APHRODITE
Goddess of love and beauty
VENUS

ATHENA
Goddess of wisdom and warfare
MINERVA

ARTEMIS
Goddess of the hunt, wilderness, and childbirth
DIANA

APOLLO
God of the sun, music, and poetry
APOLLO

ARES
God of war
MARS

HERMES
Messenger of the gods, god of trade
MERCURY

HEPHAESTUS
God of fire, metalworking, and sculpture
VULCAN

Gladiators in the Arena

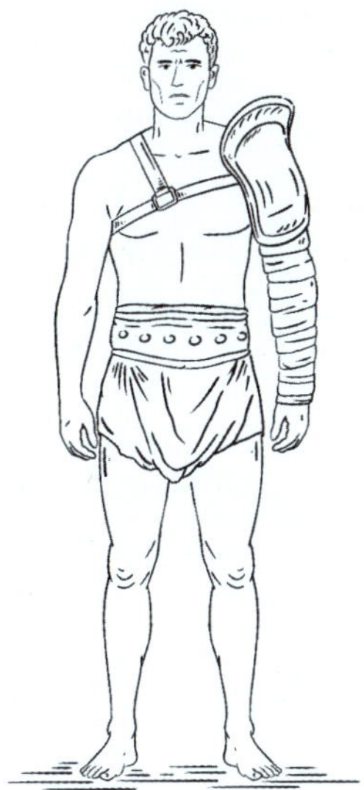

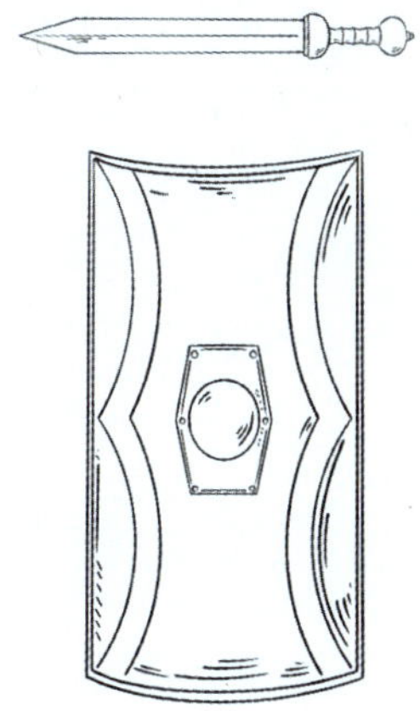

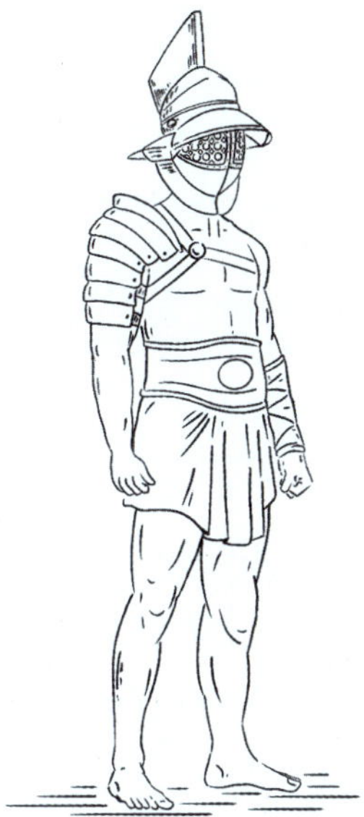

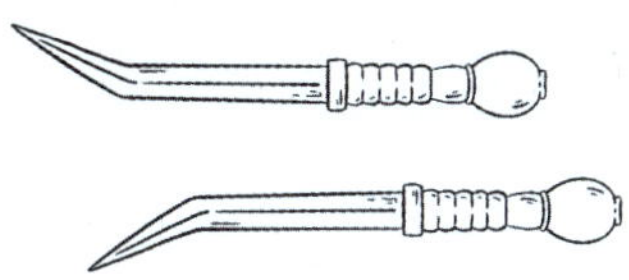

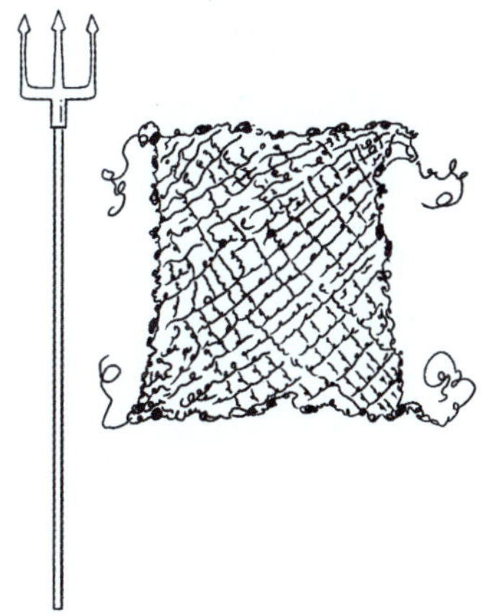

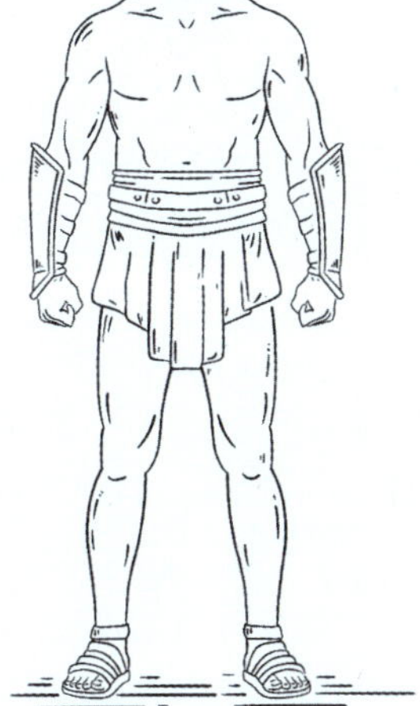

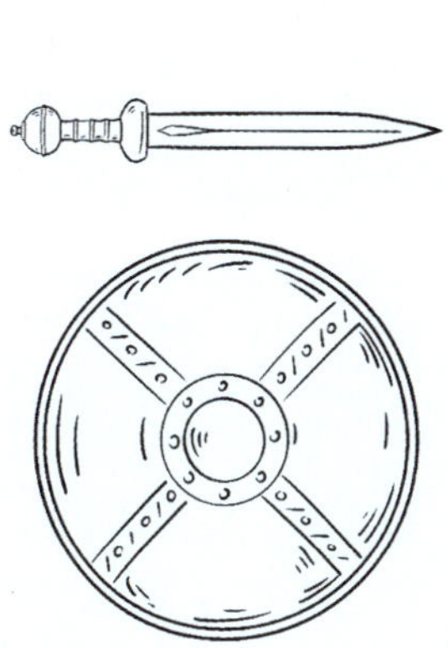

Name ______________________

Date ______________________

The Gladiator School

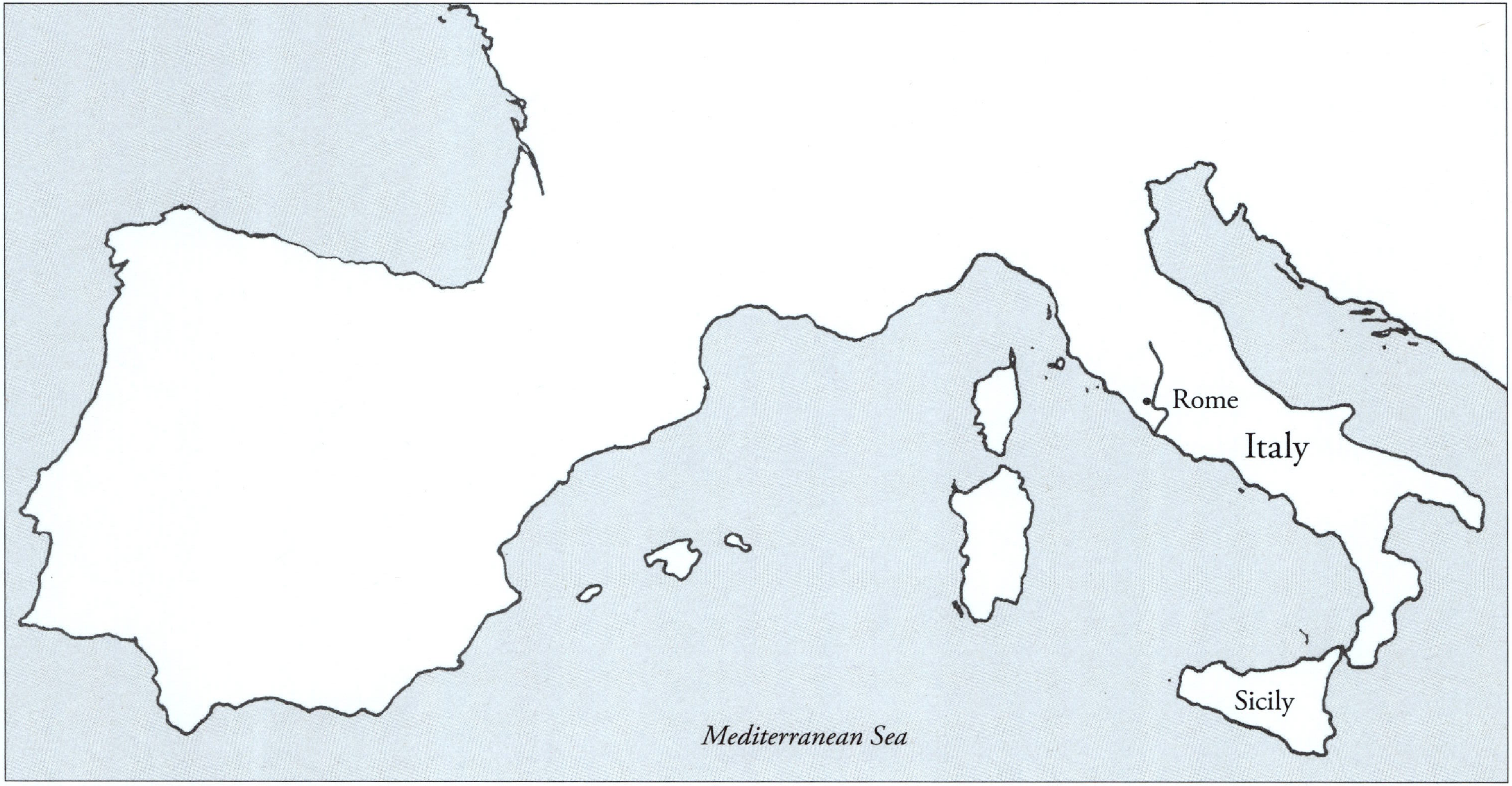

Spartacus

Name ______________________

Date ______________________

The Punic Wars

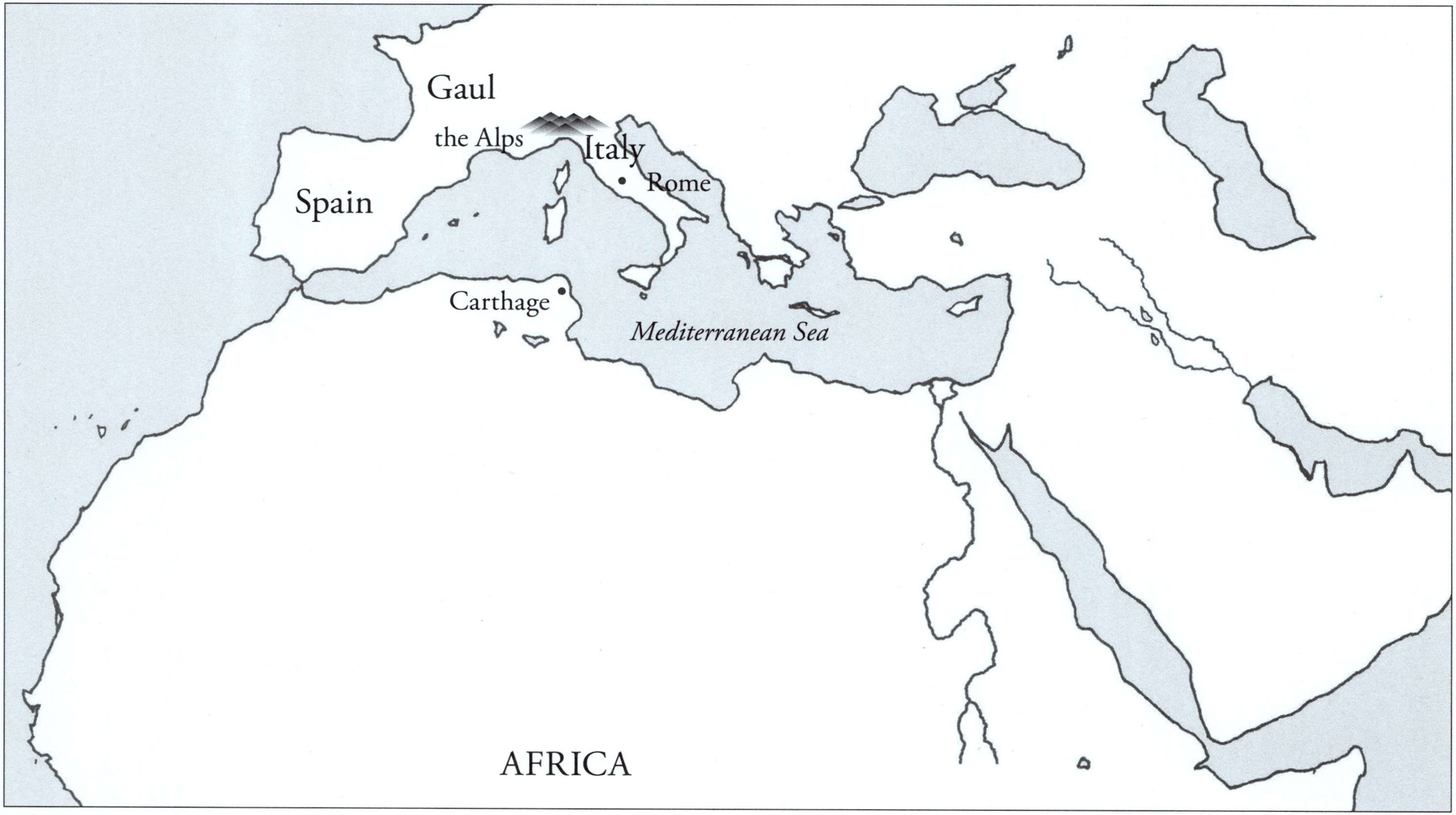

Hannibal's War Elephants

Hannibal

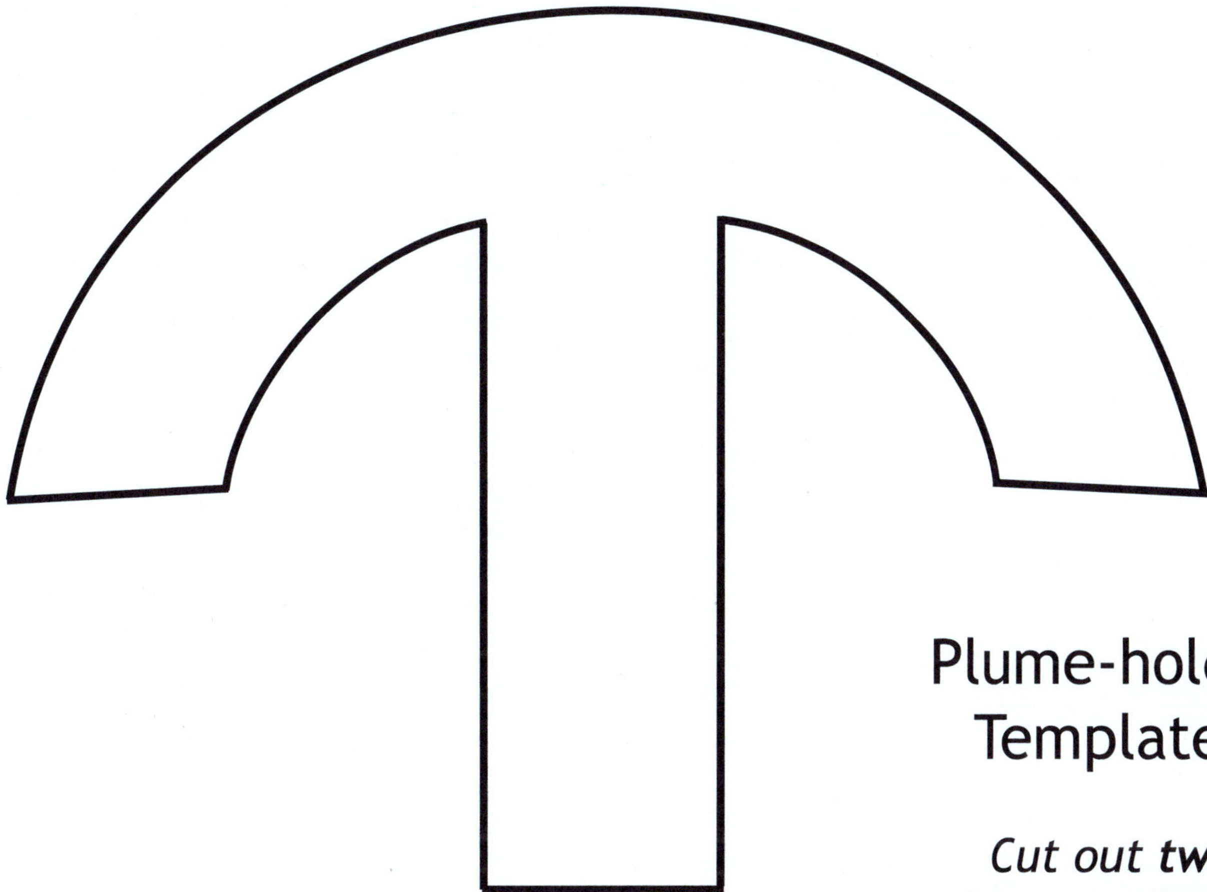

Plume-holder
Template A

*Cut out **two***
from cardboard

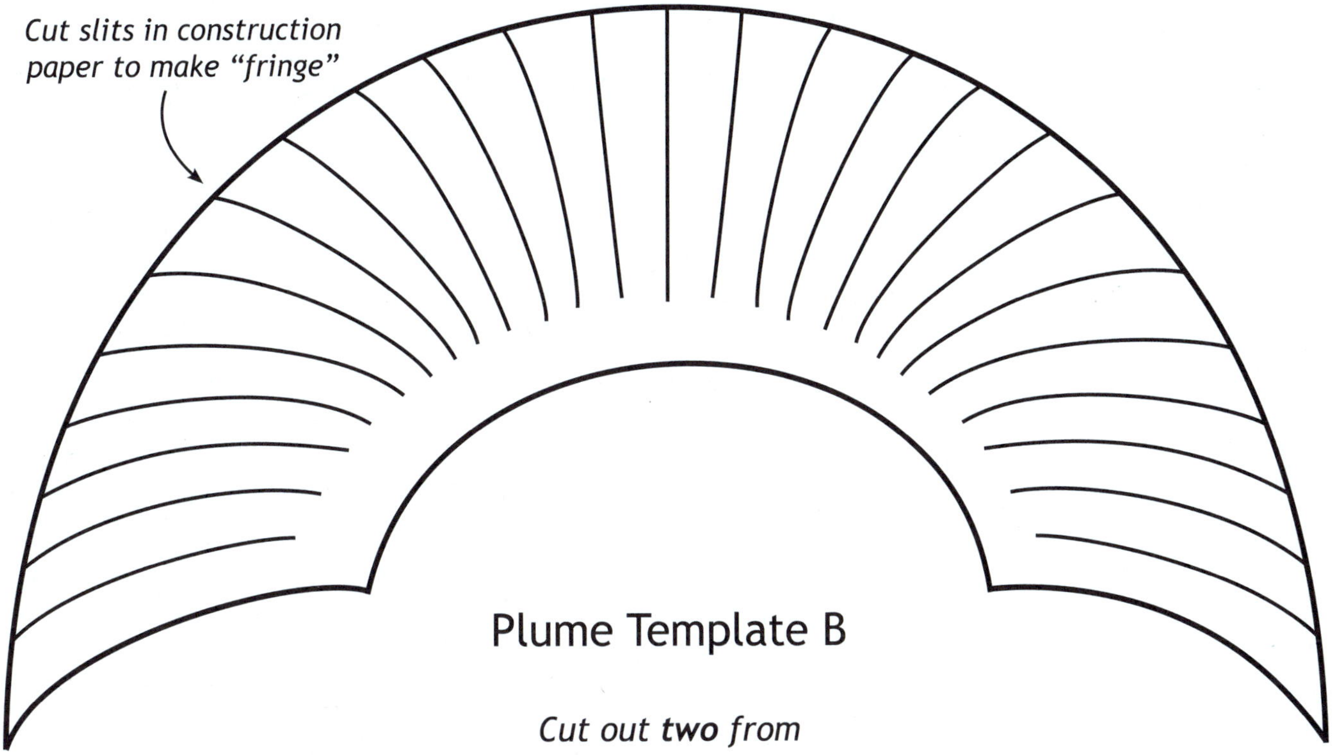

Plume Template B

Cut out ***two*** *from red construction paper*

The Great Wall of China

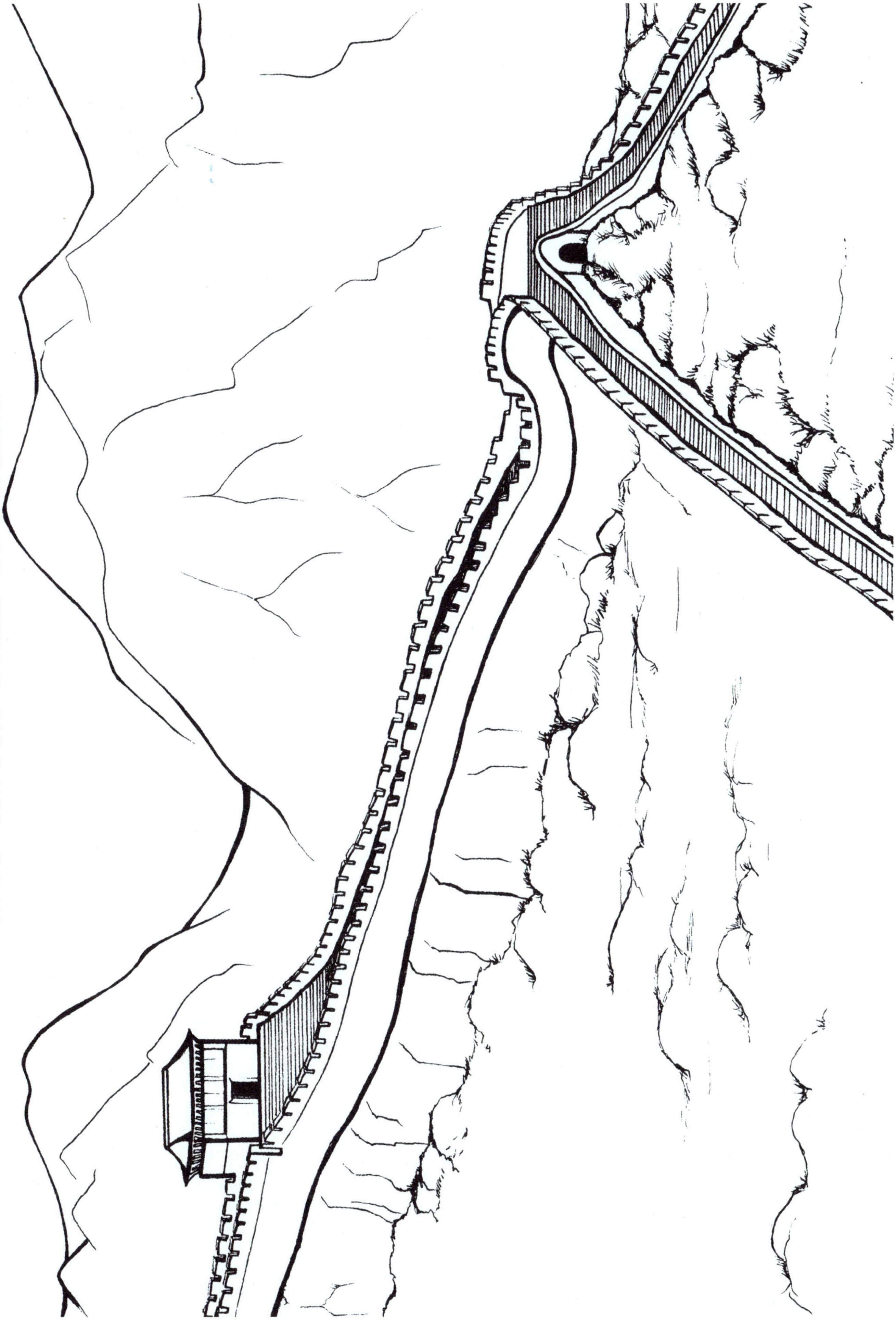

Name ____________________

Date ____________________

The First Emperor's Grave

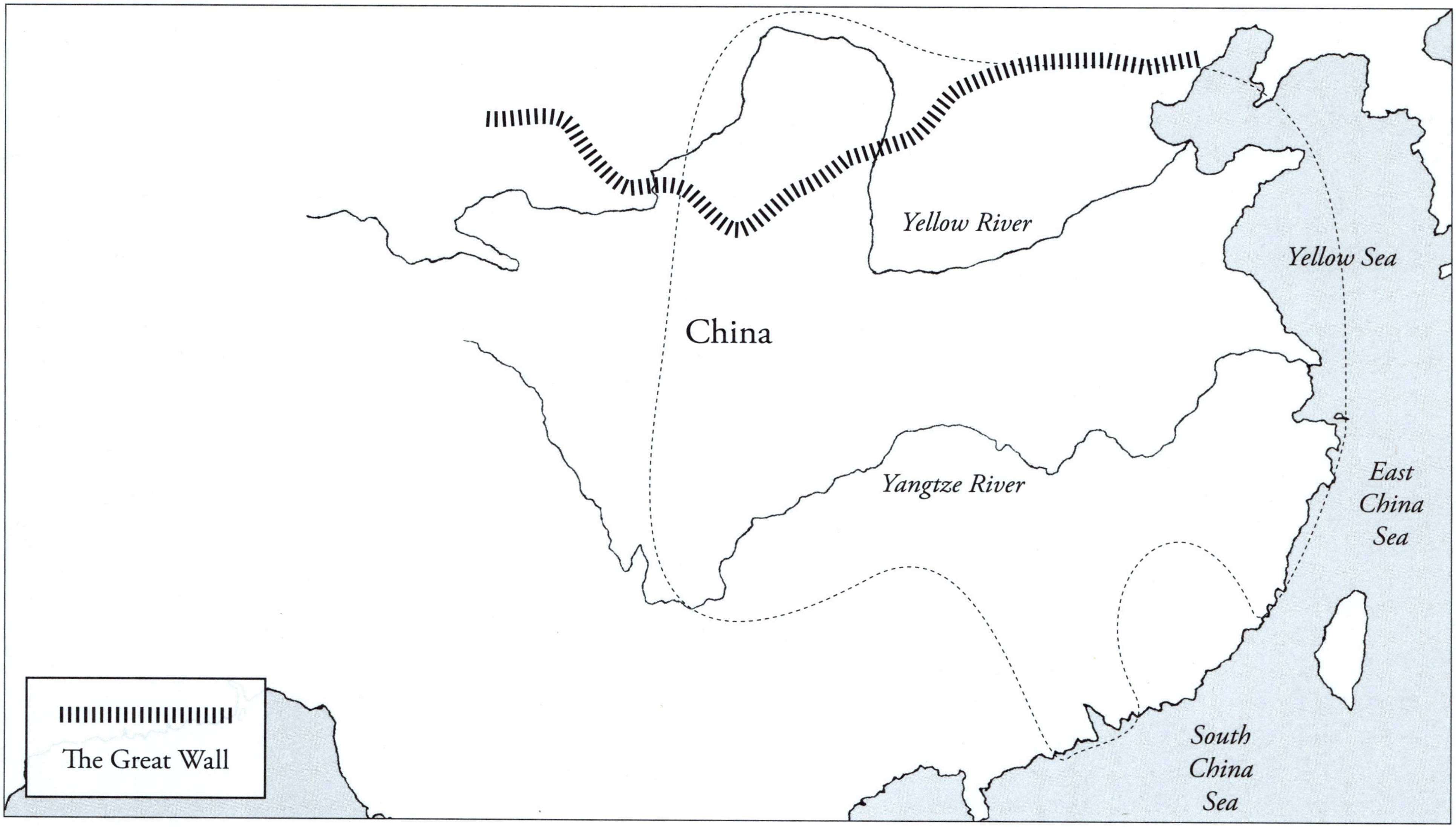

Liu Bang

Zhang Qian

Name ______________________

Date ______________________

The Rise of Julius Caesar

"Ransom Caesar" Game

4						
3						
2						
1						
	P	I	R	A	T	E

4						
3						
2						
1						
	P	I	R	A	T	E

Name ____________________

Date ____________________

Caesar Crosses the Rubicon

Julius Caesar

Name ______________________

Date ______________________

The Death of Caesar

Augustus Caesar

THE FIRST ROMAN PRINCE

Herod's Temple

Name ____________________ Date ____________

A Prophet Named Jesus

Make Your Own Dreidel

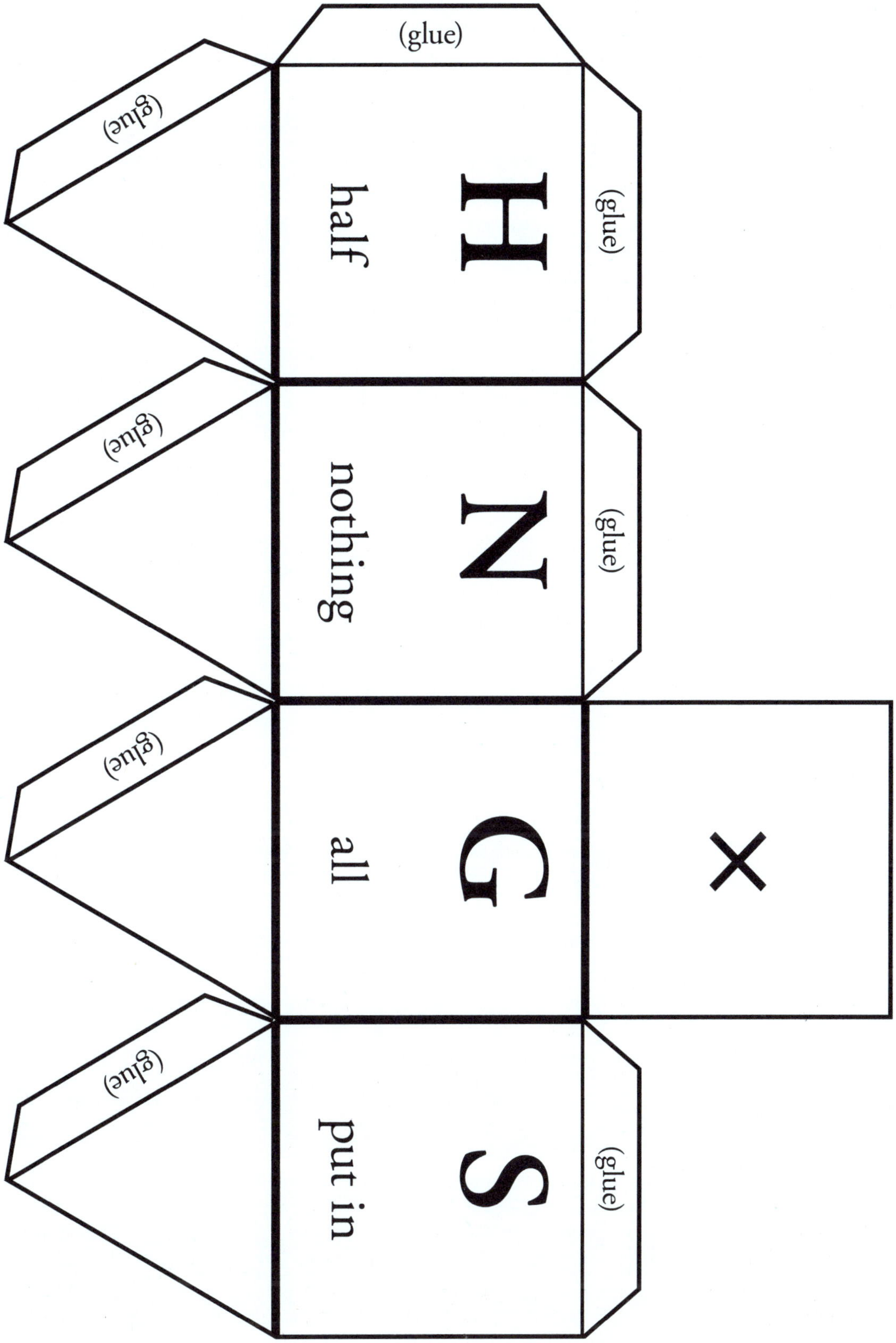

Judas Maccabee

Name ______________________________ Date ____________

Nero, the Evil Emperor

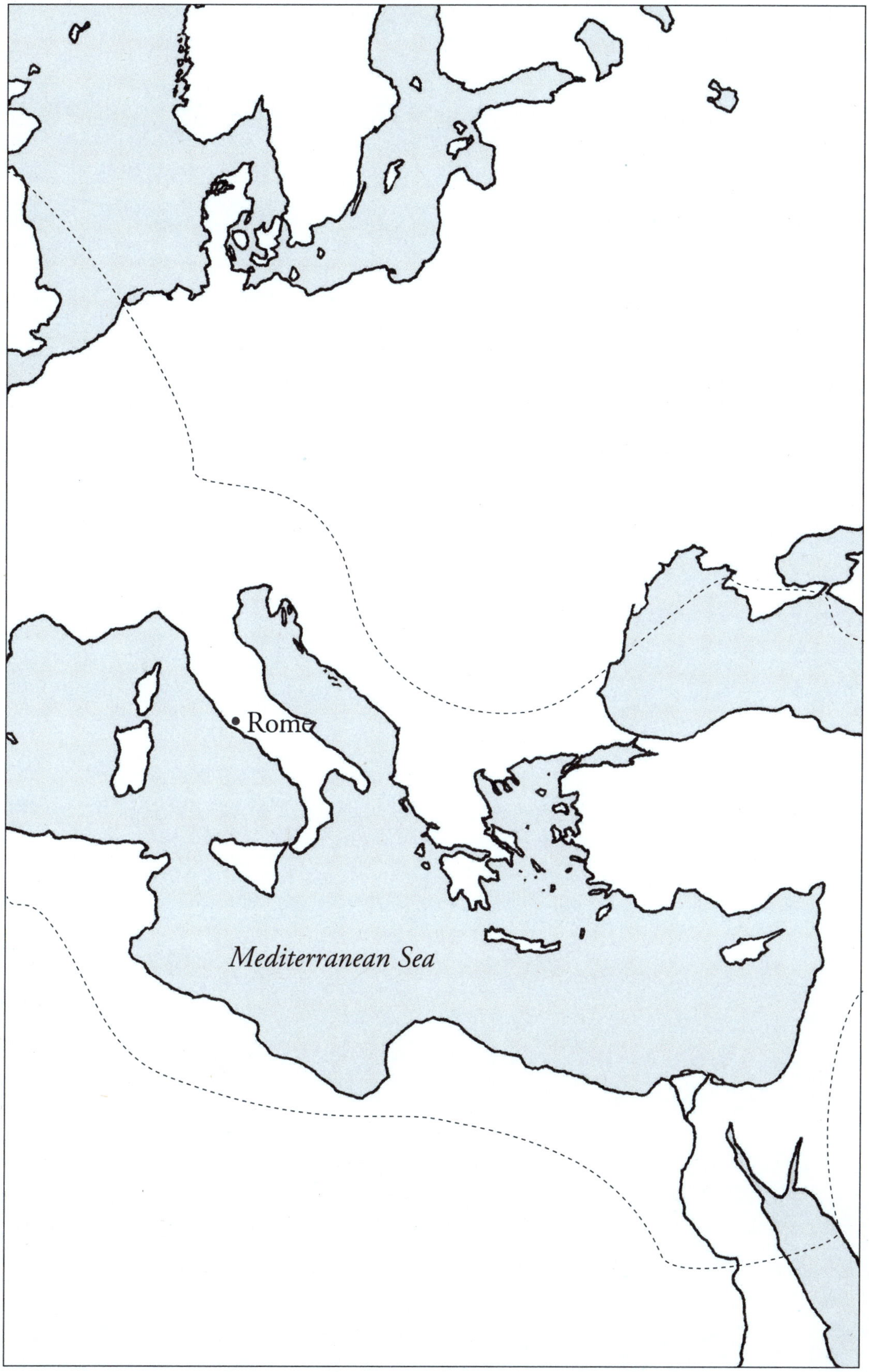

The Catacombs

Boadicea In Her Chariot

Name ______________________

Date ______________________

The British Rebellion

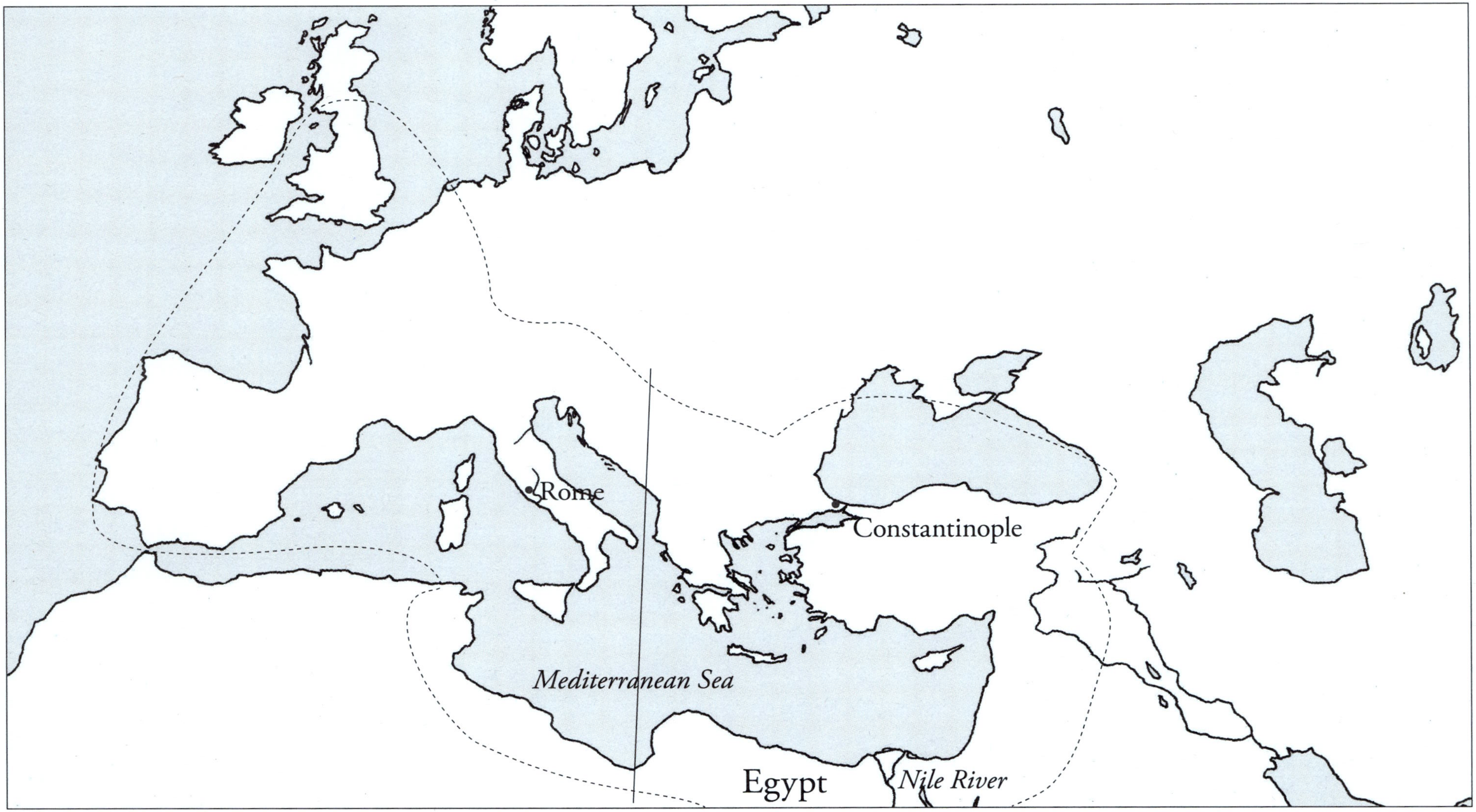

Mount Vesuvius Erupts

Name ______________________

Date ______________________

The Three Kingdoms, The Jin, and the Sixteen Kingdoms

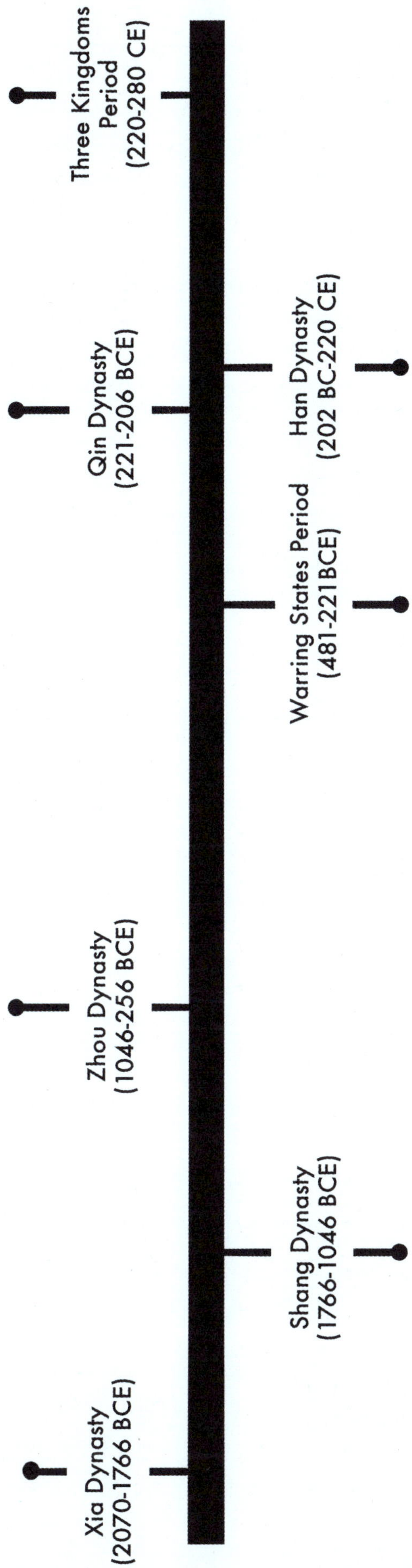
Xia Dynasty
(2070-1766 BCE)
Shang Dynasty
(1766-1046 BCE)
Zhou Dynasty
(1046-256 BCE)
Warring States Period
(481-221BCE)
Qin Dynasty
(221-206 BCE)
Han Dynasty
(202 BC-220 CE)
Three Kingdoms
Period
(220-280 CE)

Zhang Heng's Earthquake Detector

KING MICHEON
(King of Goguryeo)

KING SOSURIM
(King of Goguryeo, Micheon's Grandson)

GWANGGAETO THE EXPANDER
(King of Goguryeo, nephew of Sosurim)

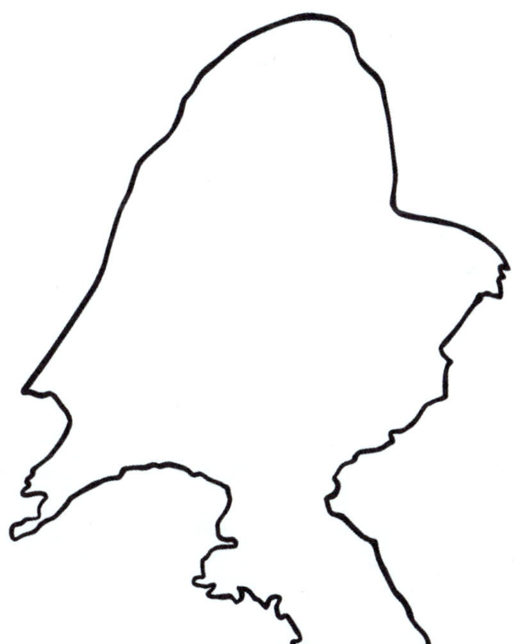

GOGURYEO

Name ______________________________ Date ____________

The Yamato of Japan

Susano

A Visigoth Invader

Name ______________________

Date ______________________

Attila the Hun

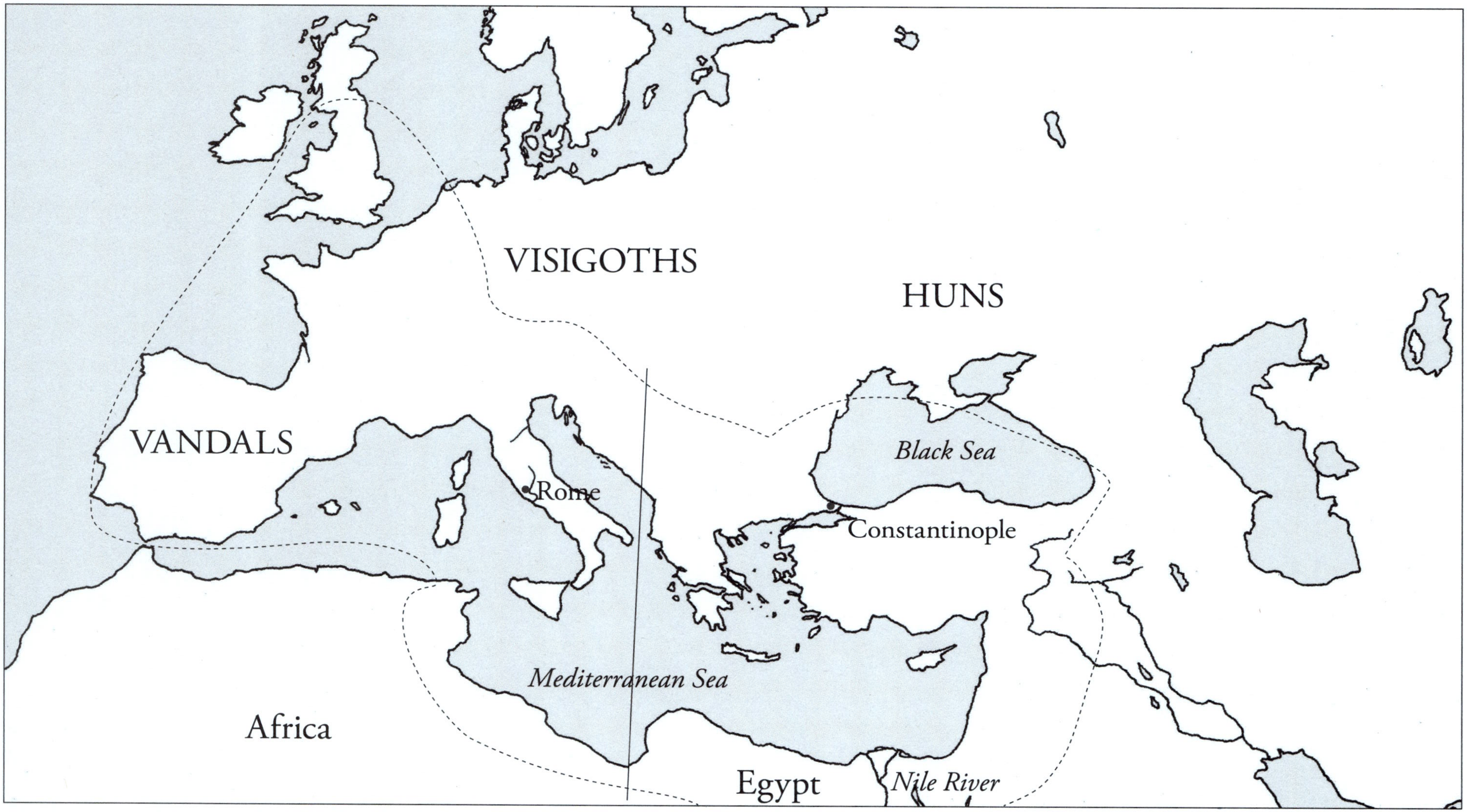

Name ______________________

Date ______________________

The Gifts of Rome

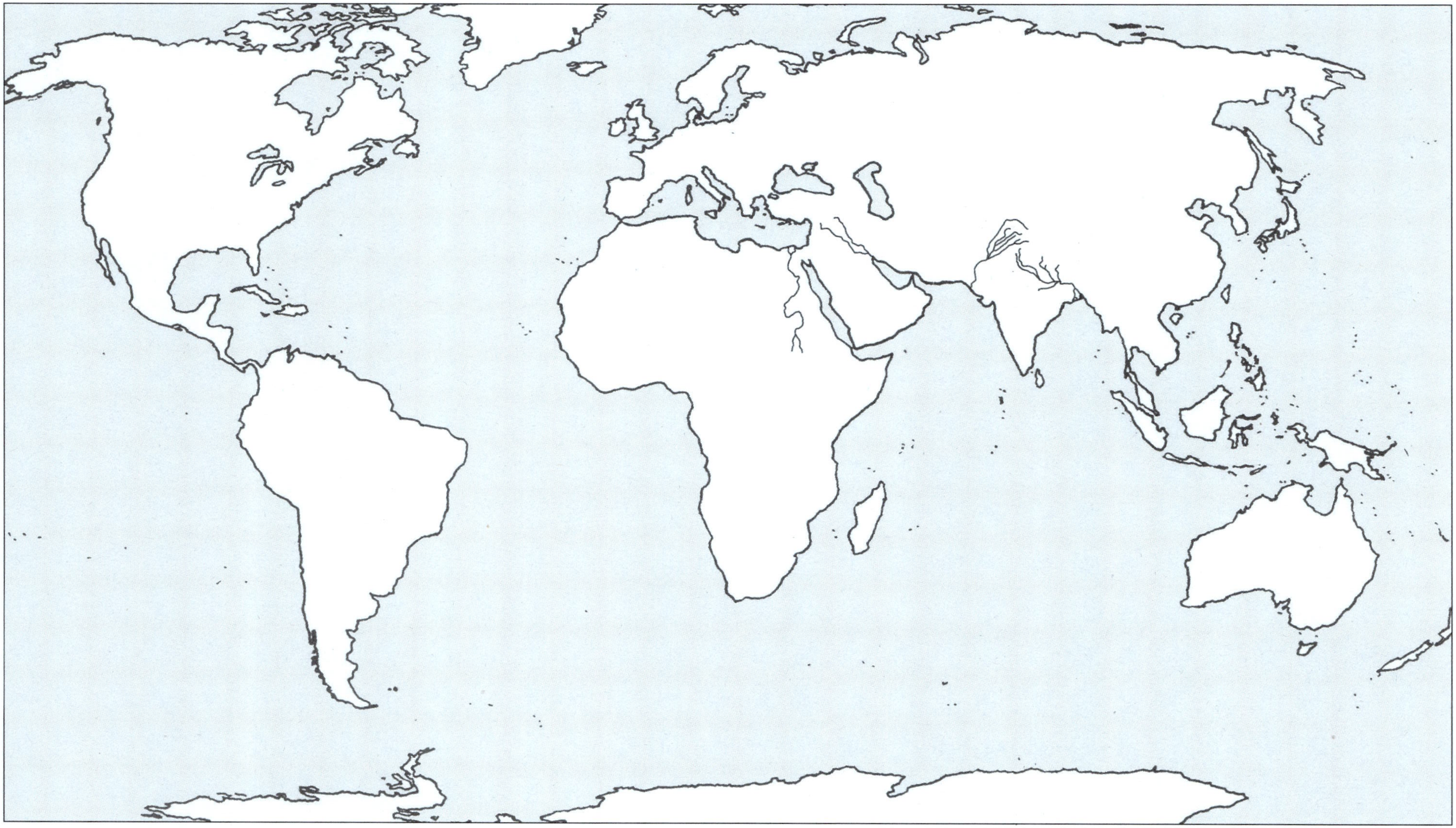

"THE GIFTS OF ROME" BINGO

Book	Roman numerals	Fountain	Planets	Aqueduct or water pipe
Latin	Apartment	Mosaic	Book	Arch
Paved road	Roman god or person	Free	Roman numerals	Columns
Dome	Mile marker	Planets	Town square or plaza	Libraries
Libraries	Public swimming pool	Twelve-month calendar	Latin	Roman god or person

Review Cards

Doing History 0 SOTW1

Historians who dig objects out of the ground are called *archaeologists*. Archaeologists discover things people left behind in old villages, sift through remains, and study ruins. Learning about history from what is left behind is called *archaeology*.

The Earliest People 1 SOTW1

One of the best places for nomads to live was in an area called the Fertile Crescent. Rich grass, wild barley, and wild wheat grew there. The nomads kept coming back to this rich place until finally they began to settle there.

Egyptians on the Nile 2 SOTW1

Two groups of Egyptians lived on the Nile, the Lower and Upper Kingdoms. King Narmer united the two kingdoms and ruled both. He put the two crowns together: the white Upper Kingdom crown inside the red Lower Kingdom's crown.

The First Writing 3 SOTW1

Egyptians wrote in stone, but the Sumerians wrote on clay tablets. Their picture writing was called *cuneiform*. Later the Egyptians learned how to make a kind of paper called *papyrus*. It was easier to write on, but didn't last as long as stones.

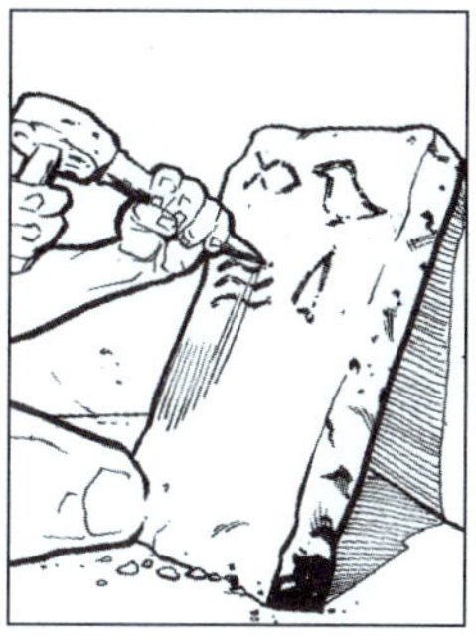

The Old Kingdom of Egypt 4 SOTW1

Cheops spent over 20 years building his pyramid, which is known as the Great Pyramid. This pyramid even has its own watch dog, a mysterious monument known as the Great Sphinx.

The First Sumerian Dictator 5 SOTW1

Like Egypt, the kingdoms of Sumeria were quarreling. One king conquered the others, the Akkadian king, Sargon. His army was strong and fearless, forcing people to pay taxes to Sargon under threat of severe punishment. This is called a *military dictatorship*.

Review Cards

The Jewish People 6 **SOTW1**

Abraham did what God told him to do. He had a son: Isaac. Isaac had a son named Jacob. Jacob had 12 sons! These 12 sons all had families of their own. Abraham's family was getting larger and larger. These 12 sons name the 12 tribes of the Jewish people.

Hammurabi / Babylonians 7 **SOTW1**

Hammurabi was a great king of Babylon. He didn't want people to obey him just because his army was strong. He wanted his empire to be governed by just laws. He wrote down all the laws in stone. Everyone had to follow these laws—rich people and poor people alike.

The Assyrians 8 **SOTW1**

The Assyrians, a powerful kingdom from the north, took over much of Mesopotamia. Both the Babylonians and the Assyrians told stories about a great, mythical king named Gilgamesh. He was part god and part man, able to lift huge stones with one hand and leap over high walls.

The First Cities of India 9 **SOTW1**

The cities in the Indus Valley were built around huge circular mounds called *citadels*. Each citadel had a stronghold in it—a place to go in case enemies attacked. All around the citadel people build their houses out of mud bricks.

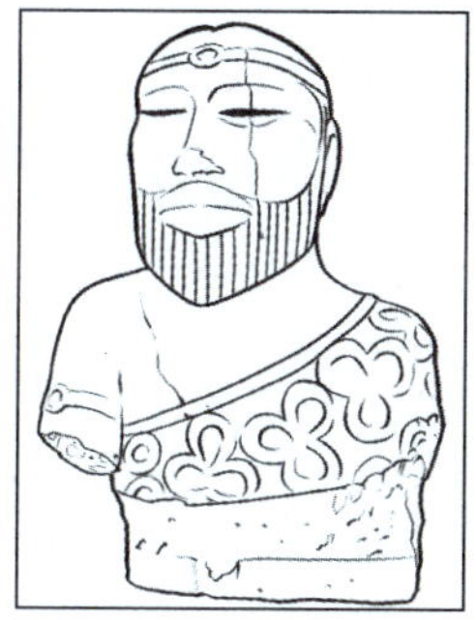

Ancient China 10 **SOTW1**

Empress Lei Zu and her court made the wonderful cloth called silk, discovered when a cocoon dropped into her tea. They fed the silk worms mulberry leaves and waited for the precious threads of silk. China soon became famous for its silk, made only there!

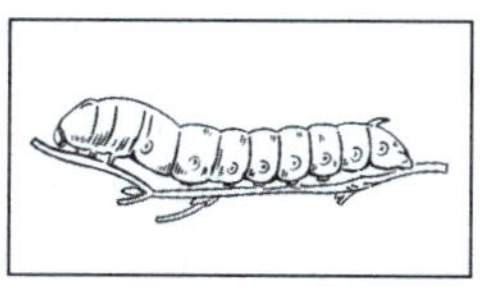

Ancient Africa 11 **SOTW1**

Long ago, the Sahara Desert was a fertile place full of water and trees. But then something happened. Rain did not fall, grass died, and the ground dried up. The people of the Sahara went south where they settled around lakes and rivers and began a new life.

Review Cards

Life in Early Crete | **12** | **SOTW1**

Crete is a long, skinny island in the Mediterranean Sea. The Minoans who lived there entertained themselves by leaping over bulls! They were also known for their shipbuilding. They made the seas safe. But they mysteriously disappeared.

The Middle Kingdom | **13** | **SOTW1**

Egyptians were overrun by the Hyksos from Canaan. They hated their Hyksos kings! Finally, a group of Egyptian princes, using the weapons of the Hyksos such as the sickle-shaped swords and chariots, drove out the Hyksos. Egypt became stronger than ever!

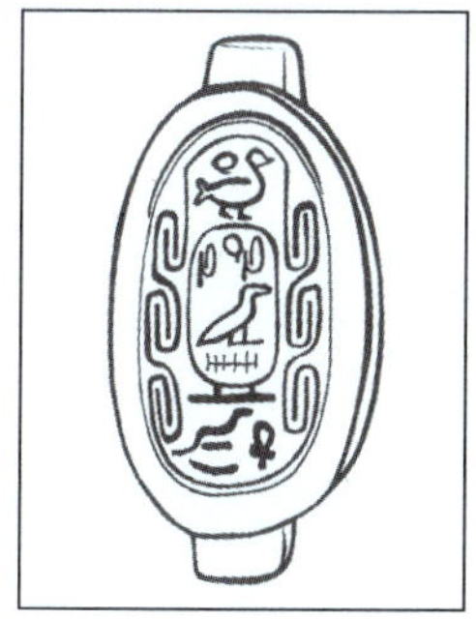

The New Kingdom of Egypt | **14** | **SOTW1**

After the Egyptians kicked out the Hyksos, Egypt became more powerful. This is called the *Golden Age of Egypt*. Many pharaohs came and went. But four of the most important ones include Thutmose I, Hatshepsut, Amenhotep, and Tutankhamen.

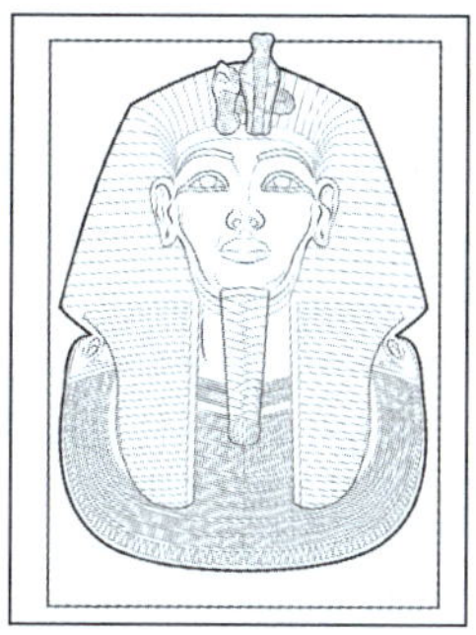

The Israelites Leave Egypt | **15** | **SOTW1**

This part of Israel's history is called the Exodus. Moses led the Jewish people away from slavery in Egypt, where they were serving the pharaoh. The Israelites moved back to Canaan and lived there for many years. In time, they became a powerful kingdom in their own right.

The Early Greeks | **16** | **SOTW1**

Crete was then taken over by the Mycenaeans from Greece. They were great fighters because they had bronze weapons and chariots. But the Barbarians and Dorians defeated them. These people didn't keep records so we call this time the Greek Dark Ages.

The Phoenicians | **17** | **SOTW1**

Northern Canaan wasn't a good place to grow food. So the Phoenicians put boats in the water and became the best sailors in the ancient world. They made beautiful purple cloth and blown glass. Carthage was founded by Dido, a famous Phoenician princess.

Review Cards

The Return of Assyria — 18 — SOTW1

The Assyrians rebelled against their masters, the Babylonians. One of the greatest Assyrian kings, Ashurbanipal, led the strong army as far as Egypt, making his nation rich. But he was not happy until he collected all the clay tablets, forming the world's first library.

Greece Gets Civilized — 19 — SOTW1

The longer the barbarians lived in Greece, the more civilized they became. They no longer wandered around looking for cities to attack. Instead, they settled into villages. They became Greeks. They used their own alphabet and began to write down stories about themselves.

Sparta and Athens — 20 — SOTW1

The Greeks all spoke the same language, dressed the same, and worshipped the same. But the Greeks didn't all obey a single king. Instead, each Greek city made its own laws. Each had its own army. Each city had its own way of living. They liked independence.

The Greek Gods — 21 — SOTW1

The Greeks believed in a whole family of gods. They were polytheists. Sometimes the gods were helpful. Other times they were cruel, such as the time the chief god, Zeus, made a golden apple that started a horrible war down on earth.

The Rise of Rome — 22 — SOTW1

At first, Rome was just a tiny village in the hills of Italy. But as it began to grow, it fought other kingdoms. From the Etruscans the Romans learned about Greek gods, painting and music, and the customs of kings, like *togas* and *fasces*, carried to show how powerful a king was.

Babylon Takes Over Again! — 23 — SOTW1

Now the Babylonians wanted revenge! Their empire was almost as big as the Assyrians'. One Babylonian king was such a famous ruler that he was known as "Nebuchadnezzar the Great." He built a beautiful mountain with gardens for his Persian wife.

Review Cards

The Medes and Persians 24 SOTW1

The Babylonians and the Medes destroyed Assyria, but they weren't in charge long! A new nation gained control under the leadership of Cyrus the Great. He was a strong warrior, but he was also a good and fair king. He was called "The Anointed of the Lord" by the Jews.

The Aryans of India 25 SOTW1

The Aryans brought in the caste system and the poor in India suffered. One man, Siddhartha, gave up his rich life to find an answer to poverty and sadness. He saw that anyone can find happiness by leading a good life. He was known as the Buddha.

Calligraphy/Confucius 26 SOTW1

At the same time that Buddha was teaching in India, another man in China was teaching the Chinese people that they too could be happy even if poor. He taught his followers to be peaceful, honest, and kind—to avoid any kind of violence, even to animals or insects.

The Wars of the Greeks 27 SOTW1

The Persians wanted Greece. The Athenians and the Spartans were furious! They decided to stop fighting each other and defend themselves against the Persians. The war lasted years and years. The Greeks finally won. Then they started fighting each other again!

Alexander the Great 28 SOTW1

Alexander had always been an unusual boy. Even as a child, he was strong and brave. Nothing scared him. He fought the Persians and took over their whole territory! He learned how to use elephants in combat. He also built cities and gave them his name.

The Mauryan Empire 29 SOTW1

The most famous Mauryan emperor was named Asoka. He conquered many cities in a war that killed thousands. When he saw the suffering the war caused, he decided to try and bring people in through honesty, truthfulness, and mercy. He followed Buddha.

Review Cards

The People of the Americas 30 **SOTW1**

The Olmecs were the first civilization in Central America. They built a city on top of a hill. At the center they built a pyramid of dirt and clay. On top of that they built their temple, with the statues of the heads of their rulers around it. They carried every bit of the dirt up in baskets!

The Roman Empire 31 **SOTW1**

The Romans needed more land so they attacked their neighbors. The more land they got, the richer they became. The cities grew larger and the people needed more fresh water. So they designed special channels for water called *aqueducts*. They also built many roads.

Rome's War with Carthage 32 **SOTW1**

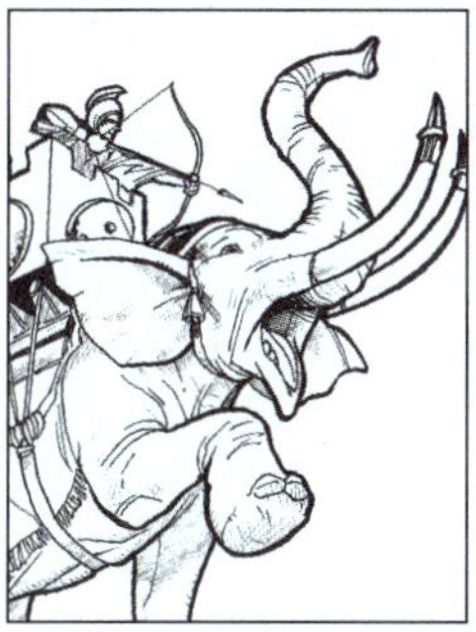

Carthage and Rome both wanted to control the trade at sea. A war broke out between them. Hannibal, from Carthage, planned a fantastic assault. He traveled over the Alps with elephants for a surprise attack. It almost worked!

The First Dynasties of China 33 **SOTW1**

The warring state to the west was called Qin. Its warlord, Qin Zheng had an army of a million. He conquered all, ruling all of China. He moved his enemies close to him, built roads, melted down weapons, and punished severely. He built the Great Wall against the Mongols.

The Rise of Julius Caesar 34 **SOTW1**

Julius Caesar wanted to be consul, but was sent to govern the Romans in Spain. He was not happy, but worked hard and was popular with the people of Rome. He went back and convinced the other consuls that he should be a consul as well. Soon the people forgot the other consuls.

Caesar, Ruler of Rome 35 **SOTW1**

Caesar set out to be a great war hero. The Senate didn't like it. Caesar became more and more powerful. He got rid of his enemies and declared himself dictator. He also established who his heir would be. The Senate finally carried out a plan to kill him.

Review Cards

Israel Under Roman Rule 36 SOTW1

Herod the Great ruled the Jewish people. He built many big projects but was unpopular. Jesus taught about God and had many followers. Jewish leaders, with Roman help, put him to death. Christians believe that after three days he rose from the dead.

Rome and the Christians 37 SOTW1

Nero was one of the worst emperors of Rome. He blamed a fire in Rome on the Christians and persecuted them. Afraid, the Christians held their meetings in underground passages. This secrecy soon made people suspicious of them.

Rome Begins to Weaken 38 SOTW1

The Roman Empire got too big. Its borders were too long for one army to protect. Diocletian asked another Roman leader to be his partner. Diocletian ruled the eastern half and Maximian ruled the western half. Now Rome had two emperors.

Troubles in China 39 SOTW1

A band of warriors called Yellow Turbans rebelled against the Han Dynasty. The Han generals who were supposed to fight the Yellow Turbans fought each other instead. General Ts'ao Ts'ao took over. The Han Dynasty ended and China fractured into three kingdoms.

Review Cards

Lands East of China **40** **SOTW1**

Korea is a peninsula. It was divided into three kingdoms that fought each other. The strongest kingdom was called Goguryeo. Japan is an island. It was ruled by many clans until one clan, the Yamato, took control and their leaders became the first emperors of all Japan.

The Attacking Barbarians **41** **SOTW1**

The Huns and the Visigoths were very powerful. Stilicho fought bravely against the barbarians even though he was half barbarian. He gave the Visigoths gold to bring about peace. But the Roman people got angry and put him to death. Later, they were sorry.

The End of Rome **42** **SOTW1**

Rome was divided. The barbarians came. The Western Empire grew weaker and the Eastern Empire wouldn't help. After the end, what did Rome leave us? Books with pages, the alphabet, words we still use, the calendar, names of our planets, swimming pools, and much more!